SUSSEX
WAR
HEROES

BEN JAMES

SUSSEX WAR HEROES

THE UNTOLD STORY OF OUR SECOND WORLD WAR SURVIVORS

FOREWORD BY DAME VERA LYNN

The History Press

To Mum, Dad and Alice

First published 2016

The History Press
The Mill, Brimscombe Port
Stroud, Gloucestershire, GL5 2QG
www.thehistorypress.co.uk

British Library Cataloguing in Publication Data.
A catalogue record for this book is available from the British Library.

ISBN 978 0 7509 6591 0

Typesetting and origination by The History Press
Printed in Great Britain

CONTENTS

Acknowledgements   6

Foreword by Dame Vera Lynn   7

Introduction   10

Arthur Ayres   Dunkirk, Deserts and Drop Zones   13

Bill Lucas DFC   Hitler, the Olympics and Me   35

Bob Morrell   To Hell and Back in the Far East   48

Shindy Perez   Surviving Auschwitz's Gas Chambers   65

John Buckeridge   Life and Death on Snakeshead Ridge   76

Jack Lyon   My Part in the Great Escape   90

Patrick Delaforce   From Gold Beach to the Gallows   107

Maurice Macey   Spitfires, Skylarks and the Caterpillar Club   126

John Akehurst DFM   The Reluctant Hero   142

Sources   158

ACKNOWLEDGEMENTS

I would like to thank a number of people for their help with making this book happen. Firstly, The History Press for agreeing to publish it and in particular Nicola Guy, Ruth Boyes and Emily Locke. For allowing me to use their photographs, I am extremely grateful to those at *The Argus*.

Special mention must go to Dame Vera Lynn for agreeing to write a foreword and her daughter Virginia for arranging it all.

Most importantly of all, thanks goes to the survivors who allowed me into their homes and offered me coffee, tea, biscuits and even whiskey. They put up with me pestering them for hours on end, asking dozens of questions about something that happened more than seventy years ago.

Some of the subjects we covered were not easy to talk about and I no doubt caused some distress by bringing up these matters. However, those I spoke to were nothing but hospitable, helpful and so incredibly modest.

I would like to thank my mother, Jane, and father, Phillip, who instilled in me an interest and passion for history and in particular for the Second World War. Finally, my partner Alice, without whom this would not have been possible. Her advice and guidance resulted in the book you are holding.

DAME VERA LYNN

FOREWORD

In the winter of 1940, at the height of the Blitz, I was still performing in London's theatres. In the West End there were air-raid shelters, sand bags outside buildings, and windows were taped to stop them from shattering. But other than that, it was a city unchanged.

The bombs fell each night, but the people of London were not going to let that stop them, they wanted to carry on as usual. People went to work, the buses ran and the restaurants and hotels remained open. There was no hysteria and no panic.

Entertainment was seen as key, with the morale of the British people vital to the war effort. So it was a busy time for me and I was in demand not only for live performances, but for radio appearances and the like. But I knew that what I was doing was important, it was more than just singing.

I was living in Barking at the time and would travel into the West End each day in my little Austin 10. I loved that car but it did have a canvas top so I would always have my tin helmet on the passenger seat just in case the air-raid sirens went.

I would park up outside the Palladium or Adelphi or wherever I was that night – you could park anywhere in London in those days – and I went to get some dinner before I would go on stage and sing. By the time I had finished the Germans would often be on their way over and I would have to make a decision. It was quite a journey home, which took me through what was known as Bomb Alley – a part of the East End regularly targeted by the Germans. So I had a rule: if I had gone through Aldgate by the time the sirens went, then I would continue home, with my tin helmet on. If I hadn't reached Aldgate, then I would turn back and return to the theatre and spend the night there. Behind the stage door there was a big thick wall, where they kept the scenery and props. I would sit behind that and I would listen to the bombing outside with the theatre night-watchman for company.

Each morning London would wake; the people would assess the damage and get on with life. There was no question of giving in; we knew we had to get through it. I have always thought of that resilience, that strength and that fighting spirit as something unique to the British. My generation had that special something in abundance, but I would like to think that if something like that happened again, the current generation would be the same.

The spirit I witnessed during the darkest days of the Blitz in London is the same that got our brave boys through their darkest days fighting in Europe, Africa and the Far East. Without this strength of mind and character I am not sure we would have made it through.

Like everyone else during the war, I wanted to do my bit. Everyone had their talents and mine happened to be singing. I had been on the stage since the age of 7 and I was well known by September 1939. But I knew I was not just singing for singing's sake any more, I knew it was more important than that.

In 1941 I began recording a regular show for the BBC called 'Sincerely Yours' and I would travel to the recording studios in Maida Vale and Piccadilly. I would sing, respond to requests from servicemen and do whatever I could for the war effort. At the time I was also receiving thousands of letters from around the world from British servicemen. They were asking for me to reply, send messages to their loved ones and give dedications on the radio. I realised how much these men must have been missing home and I made sure I replied to each and every one. With the help of my mother and another girl, who we got to help with the workload, we typed responses to all of them and had hundreds of photos of myself printed to send out.

I knew how important it was, some of these men had been away from home for four, five, six years, and just to hear from someone they could relate to meant so much to them.

But I wanted to do more, especially for those who were fighting thousands of miles from home. I had read in the newspapers about the boys fighting out in the heat in Burma and so I decided I would go there. I asked ENSA (Entertainments National Service Association) if they could arrange it for me, but they initially said no because it was too dangerous. I somehow managed to persuade them and after being made an honorary colonel – I was not allowed to go out there as a civilian – I packed my bags and set off with my pianist.

First we stopped off in Egypt, before visiting more troops in India, and then finally we reached our journey's end, Burma. It was hot, humid and the conditions were basic to say the least. But it was worth it to see the reaction of the boys out there. Some of them had not seen a woman for four or five years. Their spirits were lifted and I truly knew then the importance of what I was doing. They had been through a terrible time and many of their friends had died. The English countryside must have felt like a world away to them and there was no guarantee of when they would return.

As I was leaving, a young soldier said to me, 'Now you are here, home doesn't seem so far away'. That meant a lot and I have never forgotten it.

They were all so brave and just so grateful that I had come out to see them. They would ask about home and how we were getting on and what we were eating and simple things like that. But the sad reality was that many of them would never see home, their loved ones and families again.

In the years since I have met hundreds, if not thousands of veterans at events and commemorations. Like those in this book, they all share that incredible fighting spirit, courage and humility. They never make a big deal of what they did for this country during the war, but the fact is, if it were not for them, the world could be a very different place today.

I was a young woman at the time, but it is a period of my life I will never forget. I often think back to my experiences in Burma as it has a special place in my heart. I have always tried to help out where I can in the years since and I was awarded the Burma Star medal in 1985. I attended and performed at the Burma reunion for fifty years at the Albert Hall and they were fantastic events to be part of. The audience would be full of veterans and together we would remember the brave boys who didn't make it home. But as each year passed, I noticed a change. With each concert there would be fewer and fewer veterans and more family members taking their place. With most of the veterans of the Second World War now well into their nineties, it will not be long until they are all gone. That is why books such as this are more important than ever. We must record their stories before they are lost. We must remember them.

Dame Vera Lynn,
February 2016

INTRODUCTION

On an unremarkable December morning in 2014, I was sitting at my desk in a dark corner of *The Argus*'s Hollingbury office, cursing the limited power of the central heating. With two jumpers and a winter coat not quite managing to keep me warm, I got up to make myself a coffee when the phone went.

Many journalists will recognise the following dilemma. If I pick it up, I could be on the phone for the next twenty minutes, absorbing someone's rant about their neighbour's overgrown hedge or some other trivial matter us Brits like to moan about. On the other hand, it could be the next Watergate – or the Sussex-based equivalent.

With empty mug in shivering hand and halfway to the kitchen, my curiosity got the better of me and I ran back and answered it.

'My father has just died and I have found this incredible diary you have to come and look at,' was the gist of the conversation after the usual pleasantries.

Almost every son thinks his father is incredible – as I do mine – but as reporters up and down the country will know, what a son thinks is so fascinating about his father is usually of little or no interest to the wider public.

But being a sucker for history and hopeful this man's house would be warmer than the office, I took a punt and went for a drive to Peacehaven. Over the next couple of hours I was told John Akehurst's story. His friends and neighbours knew him as a former pub landlord who was quiet, polite and unassuming. But there was another side to him, one that the modest family man did not speak about.

Like many of his generation, with war on the horizon, he joined up. He went on to become one of the most experienced members of Bomber Command, clocking up more than 750 flying hours. Such was his talent that he was recruited for Winston Churchill's secret Special Operations Executive (SOE) and carried out covert missions across occupied Europe, including the assassination of Hitler's right-hand man

Reinhard Heydrich. He later crash-landed in Germany and went on the run for weeks before being captured. He tried to escape by jumping from a moving train, which saw him court-martialled by the Nazis and put in solitary confinement for nine months. After spending the next few years in prisoner-of-war camps across Europe, he escaped during a forced march behind the backs of the distracted guards.

His incredible story is fit for a Hollywood blockbuster. Yet his neighbours, friends and even his own family knew little, if anything, of it. And had it not been for his diary, nobody ever would.

Amazed at how such an incredible story had gone untold for seventy-odd years, I started to wonder if there might be others out there like John. Just days later I received another call, this time from Margaret Martin from the Java Far East Prisoners of War Club. She wanted to raise awareness for their work and suggested I speak to one of their local veterans who fought out in the Far East. I did not get my hopes up, having convinced myself that John's story was a one-off, and made the short drive to Bob Morrell's terraced home in Brighton.

Within minutes of sitting down, my writing hand was cramping as I struggled to keep up with his remarkable story. Just like John, here was a man who had endured almost unthinkable horrors during the war. But when he returned, he went home, found work and got on with his life. If you passed Bob in the street today, you would not give him a second glance – blissfully unaware of the physical and mental trauma he faced while fighting for our freedom.

From this point on, I knew I had to get their stories out there. I called some of my contacts and asked if they knew of any other locals who had served in the war. Within weeks I had spoken to an Auschwitz survivor, a participant in the Great Escape, a Bomber Command pilot cum Olympic athlete and one of the first soldiers through the gates of Bergen-Belsen concentration camp – and all within just a few miles of where I live. I am sure the same is true wherever you are in the country, but this book is about those from Sussex – the place I now call home.

The men and women I have met and interviewed over the last few months are both the inspiration and subject matter of this book. Because, while the Second World War is the event that brings them all together, this is not a book about war. It is not about leaders, armies, weapons and battle tactics. It is about human beings and our courage and resolve. It is about how we cope when we are pushed to our physical and mental limits, and about how we find hope when all appears to be lost. Because history is not a set of dates and figures, it is about ordinary people doing extraordinary things.

With each chapter you will be introduced to a resident of Sussex who lived through and experienced in some way the most all-encompassing total war the world has ever seen. Some of the most pivotal moments are covered, be it D-Day, the evacuation of Dunkirk or the Holocaust, and all through the eyes of those who were there on the ground.

With the interview subjects now well into their twilight years, this is likely to be the last time these personal tales are told. And so, as this incredible period passes from living memory into history, we are at a crucial point in our understanding and remembrance of the Second World War. We will soon lose our most significant primary source from one of the most destructive events of all time and this is our final opportunity to hear from those who were there.

Oral history is a powerful means of storytelling. But given the horrors that their generation faced, many found it too difficult to talk about their wartime experiences and took their stories to the grave. That is why the accounts in this book are all the more poignant.

So next time you see an old man or woman struggling across the road or getting off a bus, ask yourself what they might have done during the war. You'd be surprised.

Ben James
February 2016

ARTHUR AYRES

DUNKIRK, DESERTS AND DROP ZONES

Most of the experiences of those in this book offer a mere snapshot of the Second World War. But for Arthur Ayres, his story spans the entirety of the six-year conflict. From the beach at Dunkirk to the sands of the Western Desert and bridges of north Holland, he saw it all. But despite spending the best part of his youth trying not to be killed by the Nazis, it was an unlikely friendship with a German officer that saved his life.

Arthur joined the Territorial Army (TA) in late 1939, having become bored with his job as a plasterer. He was not someone who had been destined to join the forces from an early age, nor did he particularly want to. His dad served and was injured in the First World War, but it was hardly a family tradition.

'I'm not sure why I joined, I guess I was bored, it was one of those spur of the moment things. I remember coming back from work one day to where we were living in Mile Oak Road, Portslade, and my mum and dad were waiting for me. They said it had been on the radio that all Territorials must report to the drill hall in Brighton, which was in Queen's Square. I wasn't worried, but I was an only child so I think they were certainly anxious about what would happen to me.'

At the drill hall, Arthur's details were taken and he was issued with a helmet and gas mask and told to report back at 9 a.m. sharp the following morning. He went home for a final night in his own bed and a last home-cooked meal before he ventured into the unknown.

He recalls: 'There were no tears at the door, but I suspected my mother would break down after I left.'

When he arrived back at the drill hall, trucks were waiting to take the men to Worthing, where they would be based for the next six weeks. Arthur had been assigned to the 211 Field Park Company of the Royal Engineers, who were based at Muir House in Broadwater. There he would undertake basic training, which consisted mainly of drill on Broadwater Green and marches in full kit around Worthing. But it wasn't all bad, as Arthur, who still lives in Portslade, remembers.

'We were spoilt really; we had three meals a day served to us in the Odeon cinema by the girls there. The lads used to love that; they were all very pretty and very good to us. We used to go and lie on the beach as well when we had the chance, it was all very relaxed compared to the training that was to come.'

Arthur remembers one lazy morning in particular, the morning of Sunday, 3 September. He was on the beach at Worthing with some of the other boys, gazing out to sea, pondering what the future had in store. All of a sudden two trucks arrived to take them back to Muir House where they were told to line up. Their commanding officer, Captain Reggie Matthews, addressed them and delivered the news they had all been expecting.

'He said, "I have some grave news, England has just declared war on Germany". I remember looking down at my watch, it was 11.05 a.m. I looked at the others around me and they all looked rather worried, but we just got on with it. We were at war. It had all happened so quickly.'

After their six weeks in Worthing they were to take the train to Chard, in Somerset, for their next block of training. The girls from the Odeon cinema came to bid them farewell at the station and there were tears as well as hugs and kisses. But at the other end, their reception was not so welcoming. Their new sergeant major knew it had been easy for them so far, and he was determined to let them know it.

'He glared at us and said, "Good morning you shower of bastards, you have had a bloody holiday up until now, from now on I am going to make proper bloody soldiers of you shower. Do you understand me?" We all said loud and clear "Yes sir" and tried to keep on the right side of him. This was proper training now, we were getting ready for war.'

Arthur was based in Somerset for the next few months, where he went through battle training and was taught to use a Bren gun, the British light machine gun which doubled as a makeshift anti-aircraft gun. The training was tough, physically and mentally, but Arthur could feel himself getting fitter and stronger with each day. With numbers thin on the ground they were joined by soldiers from the Royal Engineers from Yorkshire, which led to great rivalries and friendly arguments about who had the most beautiful countryside. But with Easter 1940 just around the corner, regional rivalries would have to be put aside as they received their deployment to France.

Arthur and his pals were sent to Southampton where they boarded a ship bound for Cherbourg. They were now part of the British Expeditionary Force (BEF) with the objective of pushing the Germans back and stopping their march into France. As part of a huge convoy they made their way east, passing through many of the famous towns and battlefields of the First World War: Vernon, Pissy, Armentières. They eventually reached Bailleul, on the French-Belgian border, where Arthur was to have his first encounter with the enemy.

'I remember being in this field with my mate on the back of a truck with a Bren gun, we were on our own. I had just remarked how quiet it was when I spotted a fighter plane in the distance. Within seconds I could see it was German, I could make out the black crosses on its wings and fuselage. I gripped the gun tightly and took aim but we had a stupid order back then that we couldn't fire unless told to do so by an officer. I sent my friend to find an officer to give the order, but as he was running off, the plane began to circle me. It suddenly banked and came in low and I just waited for the chatter of its machine gun. It couldn't have missed me from where it was; I really thought that was it.

'But to my amazement, with the dark-clad pilot now visible, he leaned out of his window and waved at me. Stunned, I looked back and he was gone. To this day I have no idea what that was about, maybe he had run out of ammunition. Thankfully the officer permission rule soon changed after that.'

They continued east into Belgium where there was little resistance on the ground. Their main concern was the Luftwaffe pilots who regularly attacked from the skies. One particularly ferocious raid came as they were crossing the border into Belgium on 11 May. Their trucks were slowly navigating a windy country lane when six German Junkers JU 87s, or Stuka dive-bombers as they were more commonly known, attacked. They plummeted towards the earth in their familiar fashion before dropping their payload and pulling up sharply. Arthur went to grab his gun and open fire when an officer cried out 'You are wasting your time, take cover in the ditch'. He dived in and waited it out; hoping one of the bombs did not have his name on it. The terrifying screech as the bombers began their dive rattled his eardrums before the explosion shook every bone in his body.

'It was terrifying; I remember one fell very close to me. When it exploded it showered me with earth and small stones, but I was alright. Then, above the tremendous noise, I heard the strange sound of Scottish reel. I was amazed to see a solider sitting under a tree playing the harmonica. I don't know what he was thinking.'

Miraculously, there were no causalities from the raid, with all of the bombs landing in the fields around the convoy. They soon arrived in Zwevegem, in west Belgium, where they were ordered to dig in and hold the position at all costs against the fast-approaching German Army. This was to be Arthur's first real combat and as he looked along the line at his fellow soldiers, he wondered what was going through their minds. He then thought of the enemy he was about to face, who were perhaps not so different from him, other than the country in which they were born. 'I wondered what it would feel like to shoot and kill those fellow human beings, who happened to be the enemy, knowing they would be shooting to kill me.'

But Arthur was not about to find out. With the Germans now in sight, a dispatch rider on a motorbike came roaring up behind. 'Pack up you chaps,' he shouted, 'we are leaving; it's every man for himself. You are to make for a town on the coast called Dunkirk.'

Of course, nowadays Dunkirk is well known, synonymous with British wartime spirit and courage. But back then, Arthur had never heard of the place and certainly had no idea how to get there. With the rider revving up his engine and about to leave, Arthur shouted for directions. 'Just head for that black smoke in the sky,' was the response. Half the British Army was already at the port city awaiting evacuation. As daunting as it was, they were to head for the destruction straight ahead of them.

The men packed up and made their way back to the town of Zwevegem where they hoped to hitch a ride to Dunkirk, which was more than 50 miles away. However, all the officers had taken the vehicles, leaving them to walk to the evacuation point with the Belgian refugees.

'They looked at us as we went on our way, their grim faces full of anxiety. They made me feel as if we had let them down.'

But there was no time to ponder what ifs, with the German forces getting ever closer. The road to Dunkirk was a strange sight, littered with British supplies that had been (or were in the process of being) destroyed so the enemy could not get their hands on them. However, it did mean the men had plenty to eat and drink as they made their retreat.

'I remember there were tins of corned beef, packets of biscuits and strong navy rum. I didn't drink much, but some of the men had a bit too much. One soldier in particular had his fair share as, when a French officer appeared on horseback, he threw him off and jumped on the poor frightened animal and headed off in the direction of Dunkirk. The French officer was absolutely furious. He drew his pistol and started firing at the soldier as he galloped off. We couldn't help but laugh.'

The light soon started to fade but the men had to keep going and, as darkness set it, the black smoke above Dunkirk became a red glow in the sky. It did not look inviting, but they had no other option but to continue.

Although Dunkirk saw the BEF lose its foothold in mainland Europe, it has gone down in history as a glorious display of British spirit and an organisational triumph. Nevertheless, the scene Arthur faced as he arrived at the beach was anything but glorious. Thousands upon thousands of injured men were lined up, waiting for their transport out while German fighters swooped down and let rip with their machine guns. Stuka dive-bombers targeted ships and direct hits saw men killed in their dozens.

'It was awful. Soon after I got there I heard the sound of aircraft approaching. There was a mad panic as men tried to find cover before the clatter of their machine guns. I saw bodies falling face down in the sand, lying still in grotesque positions. A few brave souls raised their rifles and fired at the aircraft but there was little chance of them hitting anything. The planes came back over again and I could clearly see the pilots hunched over in the cockpits. They had a free run at us, there was no protection. Then came the cries for medics to attend to the dying and wounded.'

But despite the dire situation, Arthur remembers a sense of calm and order on the beach as the men queued up for the next available ship.

'They were coming in all shapes and sizes. I was amazed at the organisation; there was no pushing or rushing toward the next boat. Everyone waited their turn, nobody tried to jump the queue, it was all very British.'

Before long the Stukas were back and, as they screeched towards the beach, Arthur dived for cover. 'I saw the bombs leave the planes and saw the clouds of sand mingled with human bodies that were flung into the air as they exploded. One small boat loaded with men received a direct hit as it pulled away from the shore. Seconds later the sea was littered with pieces of timber and broken human remains. This was the first time in my life I had witnessed carnage of this nature. I felt sick.

'As the planes left, one flew in my direction. I watched in horror as the small black object left the plane and fell towards me. My heart pounding, I crouched low in the sand dune, trying to bury my head in the sand. I waited, heard the loud whine before the bomb exploded about 10 yards away. The ground shook and then there was a rush of air before pieces of shrapnel flew over my head. I got to my feet and saw the medics trying to separate the dead from the wounded, I didn't envy their gruesome task.'

With the attack over, Arthur took stock of his situation and set about deciding what he was to do next. Was he to wait in line for a ship to arrive, only to be target practice for the next attack from the Luftwaffe? Or was he to try and get out a different way?

With the familiar whine of German fighters approaching once more, his mind was made up for him, and he ran towards the harbour where a merchant ship looked to be preparing to leave.

'I ran as quick as I could and, as I approached, it started to pull out and I was left with a 6ft gap to jump in order to make it to a rope hanging down the side. I couldn't swim so if I missed it, I would be dead. I took a run-up and jumped. I managed to grab the rope and clung on for dear life. My rifle fell from my shoulder into the water. My fingers tightened on the rope and I hung on grimly. I shuddered; if I lost my grip and fell into that murky blackness I would drown. Thankfully I managed to scramble up to the top and helping hands pulled me over.'

But Arthur was not out of danger just yet, as the Stukas turned their attention to the ship, which had both English and French soldiers on board. Thankfully their bombs dropped into the water on either side and the captain set a course for the Kent coast. When one of the soldiers sighted the White Cliffs of Dover a huge cheer went up: they were finally safe. But before they could get into the harbour a Royal Navy destroyer approached and signalled with its lamps something in Morse code. To the surprise and disappointment of the men, the ship changed course and headed out west. They assumed it would instead dock in Southampton and they tried to get some sleep.

'We awoke as we approached land and I remember someone saying, "That isn't Southampton, that's Cherbourg." We had been taken back to France because we were on a foreign ship – it was registered in Scandinavia – and the authorities wouldn't let us dock in England. The British officer who met us in Cherbourg was very apologetic. We were taken to some barracks and given food and a cup of tea, which was like nectar compared to the water on the ship. Then three days later, a paddle steamer came to collect us and finally take us home.'

Between 27 May and 4 June 1940, 338,226 Allied soldiers were rescued from Dunkirk by a makeshift fleet of more than 800 vessels, including paddle steamers, private charters and fishing boats. More than 3,500 British soldiers were killed during the evacuation and many more were wounded and taken prisoner. But the huge rescue operation had saved the British Army and enabled those who were evacuated to live to fight another day – as Arthur would.

Once back in England, he regrouped with his company at Port Meadow camp near Oxford, before heading to Woodlands, a small mining town outside Doncaster, on 7 July. He spent nearly four months training there before he was posted to a Kent village called Lamberhurst, where he was billeted with five other men in a house overlooking the local golf course. With the threat of German paratroopers dropping in behind enemy lines, he was put on nightly guard duty, patrolling the course. Most evenings he could hear the bombers overhead making their way to and from London.

During his period in the village, Arthur underwent various training courses and was taught to drive trucks and motorbikes in anticipation of his next deployment. But there was also a certain amount of downtime, with regular dances held in the village pub, The Chequers Inn, which doubled up as their headquarters.

In May 1941 he was moved further east to Charing, where, along with a Welshman he called Taffy, he was put in charge of a large store of explosives being held in a chalk pit about 2 miles from the village. The pair lived on site and with a German invasion expected they were on twenty-four-hour guard.

'We rigged up an ingenious system of tripwires around the quarry, consisting of tins and a thin wire. One night about midnight we were alerted by the sound of rattling, so after grabbing our rifles we ran out into the moonlit night. Taffy grabbed my arm and pointed to what looked like helmeted figures walking slowly along. Silently we crept up the banks and cautiously approached the dark figures. "Halt, who goes there?" Taffy called. Then he started laughing. I peered into the darkness – what we had taken to be German paratroopers was a line of cows.'

It would not be the last incident at the quarry, as two weeks later – after returning from a patrol – Arthur heard an aircraft overhead. Unlike the London-bound bombers that passed most nights, this one sounded a lot lower. He gazed into the night sky, trying to spot an outline and see if it was friend or foe, when he heard the terrifying whining sound of a bomb dropping. He dived for cover, knowing that if the explosive hit the quarry it would blow a huge hole in the countryside.

'There was a heavy crump from above the quarry, closely followed by a flash of light, then came a large explosion. The ground shook and big lumps of chalk, sods of earth and grass showered down on me. Something heavy thudded down close by and shining my torch I was shocked to see it was the headless body of a cow, its shattered body lying in a gory mess.'

Thankfully the bomb had just missed the quarry and the only casualty of the raid was the poor cow.

By the end of June, Arthur was on the move again, this time to a small village called Bridge near Canterbury. Rather appropriately given the village's name, he learnt how to build pontoon bridges before being moved on to Maidstone, where he received his orders for deployment to North Africa.

Arthur was assigned new khaki kit, given all manner of injections and received talks on how to survive in the desert. In particular, the men were told not to sunbathe in the day, to steer clear of the insects (especially scorpions), and to avoid the women for fear of catching venereal diseases.

With the Allies losing the war, Churchill looked to Africa and Lieutenant General Montgomery for a victory. But with the British out in the Western Desert facing both the Germans, under Rommel, and the Italians, more troops were needed.

Following fourteen days' embarkation leave, Arthur boarded the SS *Orontes* in Liverpool on 29 May 1942. Fifteen days later they docked in Freetown, Sierra Leone, on the west coast of Africa. After five days in the harbour without getting off, they set sail for Cape Town, where for the first time in thirty days they were allowed ashore and were met on the quayside by local women bearing tea and sandwiches. For three days they rested up before sailing round the Cape of Good Hope and heading north from Durban, past Madagascar and finally anchoring at Fort Tewfik – now called Suez Port – at the southern end of the Suez Canal. It was now 22 July and it had been nearly two months since they had left Liverpool, but with the threat of U-boat attacks making the Mediterranean too dangerous, it was their only option.

At Fort Tewfik a train took them on the final leg of their epic journey to Khatatba, in Egypt, where they were based with thousands of other British soldiers. The heat was stifling and the men spent much of the middle of the day sheltering in their tents. That was if they had cleared them of the poisonous scorpions and the sand flies – which would soon be the bane of their day-to-day existence.

But they were not to stick around for long, as plans were afoot for an advance. After special desert training, Arthur was handed a new badge for his uniform, which featured a white shield with a yellow cross through it. He was now part of Montgomery's fearsome Eighth Army.

'I remember that around October there were rumours of a big offensive, but we didn't really know what it was. We were stationed near the Gurkha Regiment and they would go out on patrol each night and it was said that they came back with all sorts of macabre souvenirs, such as the fingers and ears of their victims. Around the same time a lot of tanks were passing through and the Royal Artillery lined up a great amount of guns just in front of our position.

'Darkness fell on 23 October and we settled down for the evening. But not for long. Suddenly the still of the night was shattered by the 25-pounder guns firing. The noise was deafening and as we crawled from our tents we witnessed an awesome sight. All along the ridge the night sky was lit up by the flashes of guns. It was a spectacle I will never forget. The barrage seemed to go on forever but when the guns did stop firing, the ringing in my ears lasted for several minutes. Then up ahead came the clanking of heavy tanks moving forward. The battle of El Alamein had begun.'

The Allies had been losing the war and they needed a victory to turn the tide. El Alamein was a last throw of the dice for the British in Africa, and one that those in charge knew would be costly. But if successful, the Germans would be driven off the continent, securing a key supply line for the Allies in the process.

The huge bombardment that had woken Arthur was codenamed Operation Lightfoot. More than 800 guns had rained down half a million shells and such was the ferocity of the attack, it is said the gunners' ears bled.[1] The aim was to soften up Rommel's defences before the infantry and armour pushed on, assisted by the engineers who would clear the minefields in their path.

The following morning, Arthur and the rest of his unit advanced into the unknown. Nobody knew if anyone had survived the bombardment. But almost immediately after setting off from camp, they spotted a group of Italian soldiers moving towards them. But these men were not about to fight, they had been taken prisoner.

'They were a dirty bedraggled bunch of men, seeming to have no fight left in them and they silently sank to the ground when ordered to halt.'

Arthur and his men pushed on further into the desert, the devastation of the artillery attack clear to see. 'We passed burnt-out tanks. Armoured cars and lorries, some ours, some the enemies. At times we could smell the stench of dead bodies that were still in their vehicles. It was awful. You would look in some and there would be these blackened, burnt bodies just sitting up. It was difficult to believe they were living and breathing just hours before. Poor men.'

But the battle was not over and the Royal Engineers were tasked with clearing a huge minefield – dubbed the Devil's Garden – that the Germans were sheltering behind.

'The mines were very sensitive and it was a difficult and dangerous task. We would have to prod around and if you hit something hard, you would slowly dig it out and place it on the back of a truck which would take them away to be detonated safely. One day the truck, which was packed with mines on the back, blew up. There was nothing left of the vehicle other than the burnt rubber from the tyres. All six men were blown to pieces.

'It was a very dangerous job. I remember another time I was blowing some mines up when I saw three Arabs riding camels on the ridge about 500 yards away. They rode serenely along, unaware of our presence. The corporal in charge told me to carry on, as they were too far away to come to any harm. I pressed down the plunger, there was a bright flash followed by a deafening explosion and the earth shook beneath our feet. Glancing over the top of our protective pile of sandbags I saw the three camels travelling like racehorses, disappearing in a cloud of dust. We must have given them one hell of a fright.'

Many historians see El Alamein as the turning point in the war. The intense bombardment set up the British infantry advance, and once the minefield was cleared, the armour rolled through and crushed what was left of the enemy.

The victory resulted in 30,000 German casualties, with 500 tanks destroyed, and it marked the beginning of the end for Rommel in North Africa. The Western Desert was now in British hands, the Suez Canal safe and access was secured to the Middle East and the Persian oilfields. It was a significant victory, one not lost on Churchill, who later reflected: 'Before Alamein we never had a victory. After Alamein we never had a defeat.'[2]

By the end of November, Arthur was in Benghazi, Libya, which had been abandoned by the Italians. The thrill of El Alamein was now a distant memory and the 22 year old soon became bored at his new base, thousands of miles from home. With so much free time on his hands, he took to painting after one day discovering several tins of oils. He used sandbags from the battlefield as his canvasses and one of his designs still hangs proudly in his dining room in Portslade.

But Arthur wanted to do more than paint – he wanted excitement. So when, in March 1943, a dapper young officer wearing a red beret visited the camp seeking volunteers, he jumped at the chance. The officer was from the Parachute Regiment and Arthur, along with eleven others, put himself forward. Just two days later most had dropped out, but those remaining departed for a barracks near Cairo, where after a series of medicals, they were sent for training at a camp close to Nazareth, now in Israel.

The instructors showed no mercy on the gruelling course, but Arthur was fitter than ever and passed with flying colours. It was at an airfield called Ramit David near Haifa, Israel, where he would do his first training jump. He remembers looking skyward, spellbound as four black dots dropped from a plane flying overhead. His instructor, Sergeant Tingle, assured him that nobody had died on his watch, but it did little to ease Arthur's apprehension. He was taught how to fall and roll on landing before they first practiced by jumping from a moving lorry and then from a mock fuselage. On the day of their first jump they were taken to the parachute shed and shown their chutes being packed. Then it was up to 1,000ft where he jumped with a standard stat chute, which opens on leaving the plane. Soon, Arthur was hooked.

'As I stood there by the door of the aircraft looking out into space, I felt apprehensive. But once I had jumped and felt my chute open and felt myself drifting down, I found myself enjoying the sensation.'

Over the next few days, more training followed, including night jumps, before Arthur was given his iconic red beret and blue wings. He was now one of the elite. A paratrooper, or para as they are known.

By the end of his training it was August 1943 and he was to be moved once more, this time to Sfax, in Tunisia, where he was briefed about his first operation as a para. He was to drop in with his squadron, take an enemy airfield and hold it until troops arrived in gliders. Rumours were circulating that the attack was in anticipation of the invasion of Italy. Arthur was ready, his kit checked and double-checked. But at the eleventh hour the operation was called off, apparently due to a lack of aircraft.

When the invasion of Italy was finally announced in September, Arthur was confined to the sick bay for suspected jaundice, much to his disappointment. He was left to carry out menial tasks around the base and was given time off to visit nearby Algiers and Tunis until he received the news he had been waiting for. He was to return to England, with the Allies focusing their resources on the drive to Berlin.

It had been twenty months since the SS *Orontes* sailed from Liverpool, but on 9 January 1944, Arthur finally set foot on home soil once more. He was given two weeks' leave before being told to report to Glaston, a small village in Rutland. There he was tasked with testing out new equipment for the paras, including extremely noisy motorbikes that left him unpopular with the locals. But it wasn't all work and every weekend the men went to the nearby town of Stamford to let off some steam.

'A truck was provided for transport, this became known as the "Passion Wagon" but don't ask me why. The driver would leave the town at exactly 11 p.m. and would not wait for any stragglers. The men left behind would walk back to Glaston along the railway line, which was a distance of about 10 miles. Many who started off the worse for drink were stone sober when they arrived back.'

With a number of months passing since his first parachute training, Arthur was sent on a refresher course that included jumps from a converted Whitley bomber. It was all coming back to him and his confidence grew with each day. That was until one particular jump frightened the life out of the 23 year old. He had lined up at the door of the aircraft like any other jump and shuffled himself forward. When the red light switched to green, he gently pushed himself through the door – only to catch his parachute pack on the side of the fuselage, causing him to go into a terrifying spin.

'I felt a tug as my chute opened but looking up I saw it was only partially open because my rigging lines were twisted. I realised I was falling faster than I should have been and desperately started to untwist my rigging lines as I had been taught.'

Finally the chute opened fully, just before Arthur hit the ground with a jarring thud. Pain shot up through his feet and he lay there fully expecting to have shattered his legs. Then came the reassuring voice of the medic. 'You are bloody lucky mate, you've only got a sprained ankle.'

Arthur was given a few days' leave, a time that would change his life forever. He decided to take up an invitation to join his friend and officer Lieutenant Toby Thomas, who was off to Bath to visit his mother. Two of Arthur's mates joined them and after dropping Lieutenant Thomas at his mother's house, they took the army jeep that they had been given and explored the town.

'I remember we went straight to the Woolworths where upstairs there was a coffee bar. There were these two ATS (Auxiliary Territorial Service) girls standing by the bar and one had bright red hair. One of my mates dared me to go and speak to her so I did. I said hello and bought her a drink and we got talking. We had a really nice time, but then they said they had to get back to their base. We offered them a lift in the jeep and, after stopping off at a pub on the way back, we drove straight on to the parade ground. We got in a bit of trouble for that but it was all good fun.

'It turned out she'd managed to get my contact details from her friend who had got pally with one of my mates. We started writing to each other and speaking on the phone when we could, we got on really well. Then I heard she had been taken into hospital with a glandular problem, so I hitchhiked to Bristol and I was allowed to spend the day with her. Later she was taken to a convalescent home where I spent another three days and that's when I asked her to marry me.'

Arthur and Louisa, known to her friends as Lola, got married in Birmingham in August 1944 and they remained together until she died in February 2011.

'We were very happy together, we did lots of travelling, we had a good life. And all from that chance meeting in the upstairs of a Woolworths in Bath.'

Meanwhile D-Day had been and gone and Arthur's battalion was left at home. They were disappointed at missing out but buoyed by their commanding officer's promise that their time would come. And they would not have to wait long as, now the Allies had a foothold in mainland Europe, the final preparations for Operation Market Garden – the liberation of Holland – could begin. This was the Allies' attempt to drop more than 40,000 paratroopers behind enemy lines in the Nazi-occupied country to bring about the end of the war by Christmas. It was a daring plan and relied on the British Army, which had landed in Normandy on D-Day, pushing eastwards to support them. The objective was to take a number of key strategic bridges, most notably the bridge at Arnhem, 55 miles to the south-east of Amsterdam.

'We knew there was something big on the cards but we didn't know when or where. I remember we were briefed on the lawn in front of this big grand house and we were told we would go over on the second day, because there weren't enough planes. They told us not to worry and said we would meet very little resistance. Young boys and old men they told us, that is all we would have to deal with. They said it would be a piece of cake. They said nothing about the tanks that were in the woods.'

The Allied senior commanders had been informed about Panzer tank divisions in the area both by code breakers at Bletchley Park and also by RAF aerial reconnaissance teams. But the information went no further. They refused to alter their plans and the troops on the ground knew nothing of the armour until they came under fire.[3]

Arthur went to bed the night before they were due to set off, knowing that his time had come. He was relaxed, confident and ready to put his training into action. The plan was to leave RAF Cottesmore in Rutland in the morning, but fog over the aerodrome prevented them from departing until the afternoon.

Hundreds of aircraft left bases across England throughout those two days. Arthur was taken over in a Dakota with twenty-three other paras and among his kit for the airborne invasion was, bizarrely, a folding bicycle. Once thrown from the plane, he did not see it again.

Any thought of the assignment being a piece of cake was soon quashed when they came under heavy anti-aircraft gunfire over the Dutch coast.

'It was pretty bad, but most of the men were relaxed. Some were sleeping, some reading books, I was just sitting, pondering what on earth I was doing there. The closer we got, the more resistance we encountered. There was a lot of fire from below and a lot of the planes went down in flames before the men even got to jump.

'We were told we were approaching the drop zone and we locked ourselves in and stood by the open door, waiting for the light to turn from red to green. I was second in line behind my officer, but I wasn't scared. It is difficult to explain, but I knew I had to do it so I just got on with it. To be honest being next to the open door and seeing planes being shot down around you, I just wanted to get out of there and jump as soon as possible.'

Finally, 5 miles from Arnhem over a place called Ginkel Heath, the light turned green and Arthur threw himself from the Dakota.

'Straight away we came under fire from the Germans below. Bullets whizzed past my face, it was luck really if I got hit and we couldn't return fire. The chap next to me got one and I saw his body jerk back. There was nothing we could do.

'I landed safely and the first thing we had to do was regroup and find each other. But there was a lot of smoke and haze once we got down. You couldn't see far in front of you so if you saw someone you had to shout out. If the reply came back in English you were alright, if not, you would shoot.'

Arthur found the rest of his group and they soon dealt with the German infantry around the drop zone. His division, led by Arnhem war hero John Hackett, had set up headquarters in a nearby wood and one of Arthur's first assignments was to take a young German prisoner over to their newly established base.

'I got halfway across the field with him when he dropped to his knees and started crying and screaming "no comrade" among other things. I couldn't speak German and I didn't really know what he was saying so I dragged him to his feet, prodded him and we got going again. I later found out he had been told we took no prisoners so thought I was going to the woods to shoot him.'

Arthur had survived the drop, but now came the real job of taking the bridge at Arnhem. Still 5 miles from the target, they began their advance and spent the first night in the village of Wolfheze, where they were strafed by enemy fighters. The following morning they pressed on and dug in atop a number of small hills overlooking a valley that the Germans were expected to pass through.

Sure enough, just over an hour later, a convoy trundled through with infantry and armoured cars in abundance. The paras, with the element of surprise in their favour, opened fire. But soon the advantage was lost and their casualties started to mount up. The signal for retreat was given and they were pushed back to the village of Oosterbeek, where they set up their headquarters in a large house.

The British had come up against a far greater force than anticipated and, with the rest of the army struggling to get through from France and Belgium to the west, they were soon surrounded. The Germans, supported by their Panzer divisions, moved forward and attempted to squeeze them into submission. But the order given was to hold the line.

At their new makeshift headquarters in Oosterbeek, Arthur and his unit were ordered to dig slit trenches in the garden. The Germans rained down mortar fire and attacked with infantry, but they were told to hold the position at all costs until help arrived.

'They would mortar us at the same time every morning and every night. That was one thing about the Germans, they were very methodical so we knew when the attacks would come. We lost a lot of men to the mortars though, there was very little cover in those slit trenches and it was luck really whether you survived. I remember sheltering in my trench and seeing a mortar hit the one next to us and kill the men in it. They just rained down on us; there was nothing you could really do.

'The other problem we had was with small pockets of infantry coming out the woods and surprising us. The RAF had tried to drop a load of supplies, but instead of sending us food and ammunition they sent red berets and uniforms for some reason. Of course the Germans got hold of them and they would walk quietly through the woods and we would think it was a British patrol. Then they would start firing. We would return fire but it was very difficult to tell if you had hit anyone. You would see the occasional solider fall to the ground but I had no idea if they had been wounded or killed.

'It was a really tough time, but we had to hang on in there, we had to hold the position despite the fact that we were surrounded. I remember the Germans used to try and speak to us using this loudspeaker. They would say things like "Why don't you surrender, we would look after you as prisoners of war, you don't stand a chance". Of course we took no notice of them, we would shout back "Bugger off" and that kind of thing.'

But the situation was useless with the British surrounded, the wounded piling up and supplies running out. Just a few men had managed to make it all the way to Arnhem, but despite their heroics, they were unable to hold the bridge. On 25 September, eight days after parachuting in, Arthur and his unit in Oosterbeek were told to make their retreat to the main British headquarters set up in the nearby Hotel Hartenstein. Those too badly wounded were left behind with medics.

'As darkness set in we filed along the road that led to the hotel, where we were ushered down into a large cellar. It was packed with tired, haggard-looking men, their faces showing the strain that they had been under for the past few days. Then there was a call for silence as one officer climbed on to a box and explained the arrangements.'

They were to walk through the night to the banks of the Rhine where the Canadians were waiting with folding boats to take them to the safety of the other side. It was a huge risk with the area crawling with German troops, but they had little choice. The men were told to wrap sacking around their boots to muffle their footsteps and at 9.45 p.m. the Airborne Division padre conducted a short service. Fifteen minutes later they shuffled off silently into the darkness. They moved in columns of ten, each holding the jacket of the man in front. All was going to plan when the silence was broken by a ferocious mortar attack.

They took cover by the roadside as the shells rained down on them, killing dozens. But they needed to keep moving, so when there was a slight let up in the barrage, they set off again with purpose. They were halfway to the safety of the boats when Arthur heard a groaning noise coming from the roadside. Silently, he slipped off the back of his line to investigate and to his surprise found an injured glider pilot who had been hit by the shrapnel and rubble from one of the mortars.

'His face was pretty messed up, there was blood everywhere. He was in shock but he was OK. I asked him if he could walk and he said he could so I helped him out and went to rejoin the line.'

But the men had gone. In the darkness, Arthur and the injured pilot had been left behind. The pair desperately tried to catch them up but they had lost their way and when the German mortars started again, they had no option but to take cover in a nearby house.

'I said to him, if any of these are empty then we will get in. The first house we tried the door was wide open so we went straight inside and downstairs to the cellar. There were candles, food, drink, bedding and even wine. I think the owners must have used it as an air-raid shelter. Anyway I bathed his face, we had some food and some wine and fell straight asleep. In the morning all was quiet and I ventured upstairs and looked out of the window to see what the situation was.'

Arthur peeled back the curtains only to pull them shut immediately and drop to the floor. To his horror, outside were dozens of German soldiers, just walking around and chatting casually. Slowly he tiptoed back down to the cellar where they sat in silence, hoping the soldiers would pass by. Outnumbered and hampered by the pilot's injury, it would have been foolish for them to try and fight their way out. Instead they laid low, helping themselves to the rest of the food and wine while they worked out what to do.

For some reason the soldiers did not bother checking the house and they went unnoticed for three days, until one morning a Dutchman appeared at the top of the cellar stairs. He gesticulated and muttered something in his native tongue, only to return a few minutes later with a group of soldiers. After nearly five years of fighting the Germans, Arthur was now a prisoner of war. The glider pilot, whose life he had saved, was taken off to a nearby hospital and Arthur never heard from him again. Meanwhile, he was escorted to Arnhem and thrown in a temporary prisoner-of-war camp with the rest of the captured paras.

'There were about 200 of us at the camp, it was filthy, but they treated us alright. They asked us all these questions, but I only told them what I had to. I remember there was this blackboard there with a message on it. It said something like "I am a prisoner of war, do not worry" or something like that. We had to write the message on these postcards and then they were sent home to our families. I've still got it somewhere.'

Market Garden had been a crushing defeat for the British with some 17,000 casualties and 6,000 taken prisoner. Vital intelligence about the real strength of the Germans had not been passed on, leaving the airborne troops with an impossible task of holding the bridge at Arnhem. The defeat meant it would be another eight months before the war finally ended in Europe, a time that Arthur would spend as a prisoner.

Just days after his capture, Arthur and the 200-odd paras at the temporary camp were rounded up and transported into Germany for more permanent accommodation. They were packed into cattle wagons with small windows, a bit of straw and a bucket in the corner for the men to go to the toilet.

Not long into their journey, Arthur heard a familiar drone in the skies above – it was the RAF. The fighter planes got closer and closer until the men could make out the familiar red, white and blue roundels on the wings. But as the fighters went to fly over the train, they dived towards it and opened fire – clearly unaware of the prisoners inside.

The men quickly whipped off their red berets and stuck them out the windows, waving them furiously in a bid to warn off their fellow countrymen. The planes circled above and came in for a second run. They feared the pilots had not seen them and thought that they were about to become victims of a terrible friendly fire incident. But they needn't have worried; the pilots had understood the signal just fine and swooped down to open fire on the locomotive at the front, putting the train out of action. After waiting for a replacement, they were off again, but it was two weeks before they reached their destination, Stalag XII A, near Frankfurt.

'I can remember the camp well, there were a lot of big buildings in a square and it was divided up and separated by high wire fences. There was a British section, a Russian section and one for the Americans. They treated us OK, we got food and drink but they treated the Russians terribly for some reason. Their compound was right behind us and we could hear them shouting and screaming. Their faces gaunt and grim, their bodies skeleton-like, they were clubbed to the ground, sometimes shot for the slightest misdemeanour. They didn't feed them so we would throw our bread over to them. If they caught us doing it they would shoot us.'

Before long, Arthur was transferred to another camp, Stalag IV B near Leipzig. Much bigger than the previous, it had playing fields, football and rugby pitches and even a library.

'It had all the mod cons, it was quite impressive really. Because there were quite a few former actors among the ranks, the Germans even let the British build a theatre. They made wigs out of old bits of string and even had make-up. They would put on all sorts of productions, and the Germans would come and watch. It always used to be on the opening night that the German officers had the first three rows and then we could have the rest. It was all in English mind, but they seemed to enjoy it.'

Arthur only got to see one play, *The Petrified Forest*, which was based on a 1936 film starring Humphrey Bogart, as just two months after arriving he put himself forward when there was a call for volunteers to join a working camp.

'I'm not sure why I did, but I think I must have just got bored. We were told we would get extra rations and we would get paid for the work we did, so a few of us put ourselves forward.

'I remember they took us there on a normal German train service so it was all quite comfortable. Our destination was Halle and we lived in an old factory from where we would go out into the woods or the town and do jobs for the Germans.'

Winter arrived and it was a harsh one. Heavy snow and freezing temperatures made the backbreaking manual work even harder and the resolve of the prisoners was tested. Yet comfort and support came from an unlikely source in the form of the Feldwebel – a German Army officer – who was put in charge of the twenty-odd-strong group.

He had been a farmer in Austria prior to 1939 and had got caught up in Hitler's war. Having spent time in England he could speak the language and would often sit with the men chatting about nothing in particular and sharing jokes. He even went over to the German canteen and smuggled the prisoners beer after long days at work.

'He hated Hitler, he was forced into the army along with his son, and his wife and daughter had been taken into Germany to work. He was good to us and he was a really jolly chap, we got on well with him. We used to call him Fritz, but he didn't mind, he thought it was rather funny.

'We got on with most of the officers really, they were just like us. They were called up to fight, but just for the other side. The only ones you really had to look out for were the SS, they were different. They did terrible things in the war and they would not think twice about putting a rifle butt in your back and putting the boot in. If we ever had an SS guard assigned to us we knew we were in trouble.'

The men worked Monday to Friday through the winter – they refused to work at weekends – doing all sorts of jobs, from clearing snow from Halle's roads to drilling huge holes in the ground. On their days off they would relax, read and play cards and on one weekend the Feldwebel even treated them to a trip to the cinema.

'They packed us into this theatre and the film started with the German news, with Hitler doing this and doing that. We all started booing and jeering and the guards started rushing around telling us to shut up. It was great fun. The film was some sort of romantic type of thing, all in German of course, but we added our own words.'

With the Allies advancing into Germany, they began to target Halle from the air. While the guards would rush to their air-raid shelters, the prisoners would watch from the windows as the American and British bombers flew overhead in their hundreds, before laying waste to huge parts of the city. The following morning, they would be taken to clear the debris and fill in the bomb holes. During these trips, their guards were there to protect them from the locals, who, disgusted at the aerial bombing and deaths of civilians, would throw stones and try to attack the men.

But with spring arriving the prisoners knew that the Allies were making good headway, not least because the Feldwebel kept them updated. Within weeks, they expected the British to have pushed through to Halle and liberated them. But their fortunes took a blow when one morning they were told to pack their belongings in anticipation of a forced march. Around 300 Allied prisoners from the camps in and around Halle met in the city centre and set off together, unsure of their destination.

'The Feldwebel didn't even know where we were going, we just knew that we were going further away from us being liberated, it was a real blow. There was no messing around, it was a forced march so it was a quick pace and any stragglers would soon get a rifle butt in the back.'

For two days they continued at an energy-sapping speed, sleeping in fields at night with little food or water. Once again Arthur began to get impatient, not happy with the situation he found himself in. Late on the second afternoon, with most of the prisoners dead on their feet, the guards ordered the march to a halt.

'The men just dropped where they stood, the road becoming littered with spread-eagled bodies. I lay at the side of the road looking at the green countryside merging into forest. In front of me a thick hedge separated the road from a field that rose to the edge of the forest. Then I suddenly noticed a small gap in the hedge close to where I lay. My heart began to pound as the idea struck me.'

With the guards in a huddle, Arthur casually walked up to the hedge and pretended to answer a call of nature. Then mid-act he pushed his way through the thicket and darted across the open field.

'All of a sudden I heard shouting and then they started firing. Bullets were whizzing past me so I started to zigzag across the field to make it harder for them to hit me. I was going as fast as I could and my heart was pounding. When I reached the tree line I dived into the nearest hedge.'

He lay there motionless, stifling his heavy breathing so as not to make a noise. Then came the sound of jackboots on the forest floor – he had been followed. The guards split up, with one circling the hedge he was hiding in. He covered himself as best he could, but there was nothing he could do other than pray he was not spotted. After several nerve-wracking minutes, they appeared to give up and returned to the march. But Arthur was taking no risks and waited another two hours until he was convinced they had gone. He had escaped on the spur of the moment and, having no idea where to go, he decided to try and get some sleep in a hollowed-out tree trunk.

Just minutes had passed when he heard the sound of footsteps once more. Unarmed, he peered through the branches to catch a glimpse of the uniform approaching, desperately hoping it was another escapee from the march. But it wasn't, it was a German officer. Fearing the worst, he stepped out, only to find a familiar face: it was the Feldwebel.

'He said, "Oh hello Arthur, you made it". I asked him what he was doing here and he told me that he'd had enough and had deserted. He said he was on his way to a farmer friend nearby who hated the Germans and Hitler. He said he would help me.'

The unlikely pair set off together in search of the farm, chatting about their lives and what they hoped to do next. Despite the badges on their uniforms, they were now very much on the same side and had to avoid capture at all costs. However, it soon became apparent that they weren't the only two to escape the march, when they stumbled across five British soldiers hiding in a nearby hut. Now seven, the escapees set off towards the farm.

'When we got there, we stayed back and let the Feldwebel go and do the talking. Thankfully the farmer agreed to help and he hid us in a small copse of trees in one of his fields. He brought us some straw to sleep on and he made us some soup. There were German patrols in the area and he could have got in a lot of trouble so we had to be very careful.'

For a week they camped out in the field with the farmer visiting them daily to bring food and water. But they remained at huge risk, exposed deep behind enemy lines. So when they heard the Americans shelling the German position in the distance, they realised it was their opportunity. They packed up and made their way to the farmhouse with the Feldwebel and asked which way they needed to go.

'He told us that we had to walk across this marsh, which he had marked a route through with twigs and rags. Once we got to the end, it was another 5 miles along a path to the village where the Americans were. We thanked the farmer for his help and then set off with the Feldwebel through the bog. It was slow going and then we heard a sound behind us, it was German soldiers. We were so close to freedom and we thought we would be taken prisoner again.'

The Feldwebel dropped back to investigate, but to their relief the six soldiers were also deserters and so joined the procession to the village. On their arrival, the American general in charge could hardly believe his eyes. Here was a para, leading five British soldiers, a German officer and five more German soldiers through the middle of a war zone.

The Germans were quickly ushered away by the American GIs and Arthur said his goodbyes, shook the Feldwebel by the hand and thanked him for his kindness. The pair's unlikely friendship had developed despite the uniforms they wore and the countries they had fought for. It was no doubt a bond that saved both their lives.

With the Americans advancing at speed towards Berlin, Arthur was taken back to their depot to be flown home. Following Arnhem, the rest of his unit had been redeployed to fight in Norway. But with the war seemingly drawing to a close, it was decided it was not worth sending Arthur to join them. He was instead posted to a camp on the west coast of Scotland before being moved down to Ripon. It was during his time in North Yorkshire that the Germans finally surrendered and victory in Europe was secured.

'It was good to finally get home after what had been a busy few years. I had travelled to places I never dreamed of visiting and met all kinds of people, not to mention my wife. It was a difficult few years though and I was lucky as many of those I knew did not make it.'

When Arthur caught the bus to the TA drill hall in Queen's Square back in the autumn of 1939, he was a 19-year-old plasterer. Now, returning to his parents' home in Portslade six years later, he was a battle-hardened para who had fought in Europe and North Africa. He had experienced more of the war in those few short years than most. But like so many others, he quietly went back to his old life, knowing that he had done his bit.

BILL LUCAS DFC

HITLER, THE OLYMPICS AND ME

Seb Coe, Steve Ovett and Mo Farah are regarded as the greatest middle-distance runners this country has ever produced. However, were it not for the Second World War, another name could have been added to that list: Bill Lucas. In the mid-1930s the young runner's competitive times were plummeting as he set his sights on the 1940 Helsinki Olympics and the 5,000m world record. The athlete would have been 23 at the time of the Games and in his prime. But when war was declared, he was called up and his promising track career was put on hold.

Bill, who now lives in Cowfold , has come to accept his missed opportunity. 'Hitler denied me the chance of that gold medal, so I decided to bomb him instead.'

This is the story of a would-be gold medallist, who used his frustration at missing out on the Olympics to become one of Britain's most feared Bomber Command pilots.

Born in 1917 to a solider of the First World War, it was just over twenty years before he would be fighting for King and Country himself. His father was a hero of the Great War, having won the Military Medal while serving with the Northamptonshire Regiment at Arras, France.

'He came back from the war but never really wanted to talk about it, like a lot of them that had been fighting in the trenches. He was a brave man though and had clearly been in the thick of it over in France. I was told that he just wanted to get back to normal as soon as possible and so returned to his trade as a bricklayer.'

But bricks and mortar did not interest Bill; his passion was athletics. It was not until grammar school that he started taking it seriously, when he was spotted by a coach and entered into a few local events. He performed well and before long had been signed by the Belgrave Harriers where he started to compete at a higher level.

'That was eighty years ago. I am still a member there. I'm the oldest member and longest-serving member. Being 98, that applies to nearly everything I'm in.'

Bill had caught the running bug and every spare half an hour he was down at the track training. 'It's not like it is these days; we didn't have loads of coaches and what not. But I was considered a stylish runner and I started to perform well. I was running half miles and miles so I had my sights set on the 1,500m and 5,000m races in Helsinki. I would have been in my prime then you see. I thought I could do well there and if not I perhaps would have been at my best for the 1944 Games. But the war denied me that chance, Hitler denied me my shot at a medal.'

War was declared on 3 September 1939 and just weeks later he was called up. With the realisation that his son would soon be going off to fight, Bill's father opened up about his experience in the trenches for the first time. This well and truly put Bill off the army and, with his dislike of the water ruling out the Royal Navy, only one option remained.

'I remember I was sent to a school in Croydon to be examined by a medico, who didn't seem to know very much. He poked around and prodded me, then turned to me and said, "You can't fly, you've got an enlarged heart". He was looking at me in amazement and told me I had an uneven heartbeat as well – which I still have to this day and I'm still going. I soon managed to calm him down, I said, "Yes I know I have got an enlarged heart, I am an athlete, we develop our hearts". He seemed happy enough, he told me I sounded enthusiastic and put me forward. Nobody ever said anything about my heart again.'

Following his medical, Bill was sent to Uxbridge for more tests before he was posted to RAF Wroughton in Wiltshire.

'At Wroughton training had not really started and it was instead a very social time. I got to know five men really well, we all had consecutive numbers. I can remember them now: 1255393 then 4, 5, 6 and 7. We had great fun back then. Unfortunately I was the only one to survive the war.'

Next he was sent to Torquay where he underwent ground school – the initial stages of pilot training – before being posted to RAF Burnaston, which is now East Midlands Airport, for elementary flying school. With the Battle of Britain in full swing, Bill was trained as a fighter pilot ready to fly a Spitfire or Hurricane – an exciting prospect for the 23 year old. He was posted to Montrose, on the east coast of Scotland, for the final stages of his training, but it was around this time that the German Luftwaffe was finally defeated and, with the urgent need for fighter pilots no more, Bill was sent on leave.

'After about a week or so of leave I was called up and told to report to RAF Lossiemouth, on the northern coast of Scotland. It was there that we were introduced to the Wellington bomber. We all moaned like hell. We were fighter pilots, we had just got our wings and we wanted to get going in the Spitfires and Hurricanes. The commanding officer told us what for, he said, "Bugger you lot, if you don't like it then you know what to do".'

Bill spent three months at RAF Lossiemouth learning the art of bombing – the isolated region of Scotland making it ideal for training and conducting practice bombing runs. The only down side was that the northerly location meant the aurora borealis, or Northern Lights, often made it too bright for night flying, so much so that the pilots were given special goggles to block out the mysterious green glow.

With his training finally complete in August 1941, Bill was ready for action and he was sent to RAF Honington, in Suffolk, to join up with 9 Squadron where he would await details of his first assignment.

At just 24 years of age, he was responsible for an 8.5-tonne bomber, complete with six crewmembers. His job was to fly over and raid the best-defended cities in Germany with little or no fighter support. The survival rate for Bomber Command was morale-sappingly low. Out of the 125,000 airmen that served, 55,573 died – a staggering 44.4 per cent death rate. Additionally, 8,403 were wounded and another 9,838 captured.[4]

The brave boys – and in many cases they were little more than boys – of Bomber Command had a worse chance of survival than an infantry officer in the trenches of the First World War. But as Bill sat in the mess at Honington awaiting his first operation, there was a feeling of excitement for what was to come.

'We were all very young and it was very social, very chatty and we drank a lot. We didn't really read papers that much and there was no TV. But we were excited. We were excited and nervous because Britain had to beat the Germans. We were isolated with the army being kicked out of Europe and we were fighting for our lives. We knew what we had to do. Yes we were scared. But you couldn't think about it, you had to get on with it, you had to block it out.'

Set up in 1936, Bomber Command played a key role in turning the tide of the Second World War. With their motto 'Strike Hard, Strike Sure', they hit German military and industrial targets, as well as infrastructure such as railways and ports on a near nightly basis. In charge was Air Officer Commander-in-Chief Arthur Harris, known to his men as Bomber Harris. In close communication with

Winston Churchill, he masterminded this relatively new form of warfare, which was used to devastating effect.

Bill's first mission came just days after arriving on base on 26 August 1941. Any hope of an easy first assignment was thrown out the window when he was told his target: Cologne. Germany's fourth largest city was of huge industrial importance and heavily defended. Being his first operation, he acted as second in command to experienced pilot John Baker. This was customary for the first few flights of a new pilot and it acted as a sort of apprenticeship to help transfer the skills from training into real life and death situations.

'I remember it well, I remember going out over the North Sea with probably about 150 to 200 aircraft, which was not a great deal in comparison with what was to come. It was hostile, as all the missions were, but you got through it and you got back to base and into the mess. I didn't have too much time to think about it really because I was out again a couple of days later.'

Mannheim in south-west Germany was next, and soon afterwards fast-learner Bill was considered ready for his own aircraft and crew. At a length of 60ft 10in and a wingspan of 86ft 2in, the twin-engine Wellington was the RAF's preferred medium-range bomber at the time. Its two Bristol Hercules 1,500hp engines could haul 4,500lbs of bombs over to Germany and its only real weakness was the inability to climb much past 15,000ft, leaving it vulnerable to anti-aircraft gunfire and enemy fighters.

Bill was assigned five crewmembers, who he would stay with throughout his initial tour of duty. They were a radio operator, navigator/bomb aimer, observer/nose gunner, tail gunner and a waist gunner. Despite never having met, the six would now live in each other's pockets, spending every waking hour together. Between missions there were nights out and trips to pubs and dance halls to bond, build morale and help fight off any nerves.

'We all got on very well, they were a really good group, I was very lucky. Living near Cambridge, we would often go out together into town for a good time – we wouldn't always come back together mind you. When we later moved to another base even closer to Cambridge it was a 6-mile walk back from town and I did that a few times I can tell you. I'm not sure if it is still there but we always used to go to a pub called The Castle and then there was Dorothy's Cafe, which we went to because there was a dance hall. It was a good time.'

Not only did this precious downtime give them a chance to relax and enjoy each other's company away from being shot at, it gave them the opportunity to meet the local women.

'We were always very popular in our uniforms; they liked their Royal Air Force boys. I remember even from my early days that they would come over and have drinks with us.'

Back at work the operations came thick and fast, and Bill was sent out two, sometimes three, nights a week. His first as lead pilot, on 7 September, was a bombing run targeting the docks at Boulogne on the French coast. Just three days later he was off to Turin, northern Italy, to target the city's car manufacturers, which had started building enemy aircraft. Their heavy payload just got them over the Alps, but strike hard and strike sure they did, destroying their target with deadly accuracy. Two days later they were out over Frankfurt, three days after that Hamburg, followed by Genoa.

The raids were relentless, the risk enormous, but Bill and his crew got on with the job in hand. They knew their prognosis and were reminded daily of their limited life expectancy. After returning from a raid they would see staff clearing the belongings of airmen never to return. The following morning at breakfast, they would be greeted by empty seats, sometimes empty tables. Death was a daily business in Bomber Command and for the crews it was a case of when, rather than if.

With each operation they needed to be on their guard as soon as the south coast of England was behind them. Enemy fighters could come from seemingly nowhere and anti-aircraft gun placements were stationed along the coastline of mainland Europe. However, the most dangerous part of any sortie was always when approaching the target.

As the hundreds of aircraft approached German cities at 14,000ft, sirens below would sound and the searchlights would fire up, illuminating the night sky. Then came the rattle and the deep thump of the dozens of anti-aircraft guns firing twenty rounds each a minute. Just one was capable of bringing down an aircraft and its crew.

'It was very frightening, but you had to keep going and get on with it. It was luck really whether you got through. It was completely dark except for the searchlights, but you could see these puffs all around and you could smell the cordite from the explosives, that's when you knew it was close. A near miss would shake the plane, but if you were hit you had no chance. I always tried to move around to avoid the searchlights, but you had hundreds of other planes alongside you. They were close, but it was dark so you couldn't really see them, but you knew they were there. You would see the ones that had been hit though, they would go down in flames.'

As a pilot, Bill's job was to avoid the searchlights, while trying to keep the plane as steady as possible approaching the target to give the bomb aimer a chance. The searchlight operators would scan the sky trying to spot one of the bombers – and if they caught you, your chances were slim.

'I remember one spotted me once and then five or six all swung around and illuminated the cockpit. I was a target for all the guns and they took aim, probably dozens of them. I had to dive and fast and I started doing all sorts of aerobatics. The crew wouldn't have known much about it, but they would have been thrown around the aircraft. I had to get out of their sights. That happened a few times. It was frightening but you had to hold your nerve, if you didn't then you wouldn't make it home.'

When over a big city like Berlin or Cologne, Bill could be in range of the guns and lights for fifteen to twenty minutes. But while furiously ducking and weaving and avoiding the hundreds of planes around him, he also had to find and hit his target.

'In the early days we didn't have many navigational aids other than a map. You relied on your navigator. The final run towards the target was the most dangerous because you had to keep the plane steady. After you had dropped your bombs you got out of there as quickly as possible.'

If the crew had survived the target zone, there was still a long way to go before they were back in the mess. On the way home they were regularly intercepted by night fighters, often Messerschmitts or Junkers, that had been scrambled following the raid. Usually hunting in small groups, these nimble and light aircraft could easily outmanoeuvre the heavy Wellingtons.

'They were a real danger, especially at night. You wouldn't see them until they were on you. They were capable of coming up from underneath and shooting up at you. You had to do your best to move about and hope your gunner could get a shot at them.

'But I can tell you now, nobody panicked in my plane, we all stayed calm. My crew could be as nervous as they wanted, but they didn't panic. I certainly couldn't, I had to get them all home. We all had our jobs to do and we just did them, we had to. Yes, we were all scared but you got used to it once you had done a few trips. You had to be blasé about it almost. Those who got fits of the nerves were taken off and they were called LMF: lacking moral fibre. That was the equivalent of turning your back on the trenches in the First World War; you just didn't do it.'

Any crewmember who broke under the strain of the relentless daily hell of bombing runs was branded as LMF. Usually de-ranked, they would be taken off flying duties, given menial tasks and often removed from the squadron. But despite the immense stress they were all under, this happened to surprisingly few.

One of Bill's closest shaves came when he was returning from a raid on Stettin, now Szczecin, in Poland. He was intercepted by a night fighter and a round pierced his fuel tank. With his dials showing the tank as empty, he began losing altitude over the North Sea. His engineer did what he could, but with seemingly no other option, Bill prepared to ditch the bomber into the water.

'Nobody wants to do that, but there was nothing else I could do. It is possible to land on the water and survive, just look at the pilot a few years ago who landed the civilian aircraft on the water in New York. I would have had to get the landing perfect. If so, the aircraft would have stayed afloat and we could have got the dinghy out, as you cannot afford to get wet in those situations. If you did you didn't survive very long. You perhaps have two hours.'

But with the plane plummeting towards the sea, against the odds he somehow found more power and managed to reach the east coast of England. Running on empty, Bill tried to keep the bomber level as he approached one of the designated emergency landing airfields in Suffolk. Miraculously he brought the plane down without incident and handed it over to the ground crew.

But it was not just the enemy they had to contend with; primitive navigational and flying aids meant that many lives were lost due to bad weather. During one of his final missions of the war, fog almost cost Bill his life as he came in to land.

'It was very thick; I could hardly see a thing. I had made my approach three times already and pulled up at the last moment, but I had to get it down. I didn't want to come up short because I would have hit the perimeter fence and so as a result I left it too late.'

The aircraft overshot the runway with the front wheels plunging into a ditch and flipping the bomber upside-down.

'We were trapped in there; the fear was that it would catch on fire but thankfully they got us out quickly. I nearly lost my life that day.'

In late 1941, having shown great skill as a pilot of the two-engine Wellington, Bill was persuaded to retrain for the RAF's first four-engine bomber, the Stirling. Larger, faster, and with three times the bomb capacity of the Wellington, it was billed as the future of Bomber Command.

After a few months of training, he arrived with his crew at 15 Squadron, RAF Wyton, Cambridgeshire, in December 1941. It was around this time that Bomber Harris opted to increase the intensity of Bomber Command's attacks. He had approached Churchill with an idea he thought would not only crush German industry, but also the country's morale. He proposed sending 1,000 bombers on a single night raid to lay waste to multiple military and industrial targets across a city. Churchill gave the green light and Harris set about raising the numbers.[5]

At the time he only had just over 400 trained crews ready for action, and so was forced to draft in instructors and even men yet to pass their training. The raid was unprecedented and nothing of this scale had ever been attempted before, with previously just a few hundred bombers making up the largest operations. But with advances in radar and navigational aids, Harris deemed it viable and safe.[6]

One of the main concerns had been the possibility of collisions, with so many bulky bombers occupying the same airspace. To try and minimise the risk, each pilot was allocated a height band and time slot.

'I remember that raid very well; it was quite something to be part of. It was always a bit nervy when you knew there were so many other bombers around you. We got the usual flak, but we got the job done and got out without incident.'

The bombing party dropped an incredible 1,455 tonnes of explosives on Cologne, two-thirds of which were incendiaries. German records show that some 2,500 fires were started that night, leaving emergency services at breaking point. More than 16,000 buildings were destroyed with many tens of thousands more damaged, including churches, railway stations, banks, hospitals, cinemas and barracks. Nearly 500 people were killed, most of them civilians. Churchill had told Harris he was prepared to lose 100 aircrew of the 1,047 that took off that night. By the morning just 41 had not returned and it was deemed an overwhelming success.[7]

Two nights later Bill and his crew were out again on the second 1,000 bomber raid, this time to Essen, followed by a third to the same city just days later. Bill was gaining experience with each assignment and by the summer of 1942 he had one of the best records in Bomber Command and was regarded as one of their most skilled pilots. But with his forty-one missions exceeding the standard thirty for a tour, he was taken off operational duties and sent to RAF Kinloss to train new bomber pilots.

'I wasn't going to miss the operations over Germany, but I was going to miss my crew. They had been with me throughout my time and we had all become very close. Because I was older than them, I was like a father figure and I helped them out where I could. Nobody had lost their heads and we had all made it through, but with them still having a few more operations before they finished their tour, they were handed over to another pilot.'

Bill said his goodbyes and moved up to the north coast of Scotland. But just days into his new job came the most terrible news.

'I remember it well; someone from the squadron must have come up to tell me. They had been shot down, all dead. I don't know the details, but I understand they were with an inexperienced pilot. I tried not to think about it too much, I had to worry about myself.'

Until just a few years ago Bill had believed that all of his crew had perished in the crash. Remarkably however, an article in the *Sunday Telegraph* helped prove otherwise.

'There was a picture in the paper of my crew. Shortly after it was published I had a call from a young lad who said he had seen it and thought one of the crewmembers was his grandfather. I said "Yes, Jack Taylor, he was shot down in the war" and he said "Oh no he wasn't". It turned out that Jack had been taken off the morning of the operation and never went out with them. He survived and lived in the same town as me after the war – unbeknown to both of us. We then both lived near Horsham and one of his children lives just 5 miles down the road on the A272. He passed away before I learnt the truth.'

At RAF Kinloss, Bill was hoping for an easier, less nerve-wracking time. But this was not the case. As an instructor, he had to sit alongside trainee pilots in the cockpit as they got to grips with the RAF's bombers. There were no twin controls and so if they decided to do something stupid, then that was it.

'There were some difficult, rather hairy moments that's for sure. But I had a good time up in Scotland, we had lots of visitors like singers and entertainers and there was a good social crowd.'

He spent two years on the north coast, training the next generation of pilots. But in 1944 the heads of Bomber Command came looking for him. They wanted to introduce a faster, lighter and more manoeuvrable bomber to their current stock. They wanted an aircraft that could go in higher, out of reach of the anti-aircraft guns, to guide the main bombing party over the target. They had found this with the new de Havilland Mosquito. The aircraft was halfway between a fighter and a bomber, and with Bill having trained for both, he was a perfect choice of pilot.

'It was all completely new so it took a few months of training, but I soon got used to it. It just took a very light touch compared to the Wellington and Stirling. It was much faster and could go to a far greater height that put us out of reach of a lot of the guns. I liked the Mosquito a lot.'

In September 1944 he was posted to 162 Squadron at RAF Bourn, just west of Cambridge. Again the raids came thick and fast, and he had carried out forty before the end of the war, just over seven months later. His flight log shows operations over Frankfurt, Nuremberg, Hannover, Magdeburg and no less than fourteen runs over Berlin. However, on many of these sorties with the Mosquito, he did not drop a single bomb. Instead he dropped flares.

Bill was sent in ahead of the main bombing party, dropping flares along the way for those behind to follow. Once he reached the target, he would light it up with another flare. All the bombing party would need to do was drop their load on the marker.

The tactic worked well towards the end of the war and ensured a much better hit rate – which also saw fewer civilian deaths. And when not guiding the way for others, Bill would take the Mosquito out on what were called siren raids. These were carried out when the weather was too bad for the larger bombers, and usually involved the Mosquitoes dropping a handful of bombs on targets across Germany in just one night. The aim was to keep the enemy on the back foot and stall their recovery before the next big raid.

The Mosquitoes were also used as diversionary bombers on the night of huge raids that saw many hundreds of aircraft fly over to Germany. Bill was involved in perhaps the biggest and most controversial of them all – Dresden. Across four raids between 13 and 15 February 1945, the RAF and the United States Army Air Force dropped more than 3,900 tonnes of high explosive and incendiary bombs on the great cultural city. The bombing resulted in a firestorm, which destroyed 1,600 acres of the city centre with an estimated 25,000 civilian deaths.

Bill did not drop on Dresden, but instead his Mosquito dropped on other nearby targets to draw away German fighters from the main party. Bomber Command faced fierce criticism for the attack on Dresden, which the Germans described as a terror bombing. Critics argue there was little consideration for the civilian population and the widespread killing was aimed solely at crushing German morale. Bomber Harris argued it was a coordinated and well-executed attack on German industry, designed to bring an end to the war.

Bill agrees. 'Forget all this business of mass bombing. We always had targets throughout the war and they were strategic targets. We didn't just go and bomb anywhere. If the weather was bad and you had to turn back or if you couldn't find your target then you would drop your bombs, you would never come back with them, but we always had targets. We never had orders to bomb civilian targets, not even with Dresden. If you are told otherwise then it is wrong. We have had a lot of misleading programmes on TV blaming Bomber Harris, but they are all completely wrong.'

Bill flew his last mission on 25 April 1945, taking his tally for the war to eighty-one – one of the highest in Bomber Command. It is estimated that just one in six made it through their first tour of duty, which was thirty missions, while just one in forty saw out their second. Against the odds Bill had survived and, following the German surrender, he returned to his wife, who he had married in 1944.

For his bravery he was mentioned in dispatches and also received the Distinguished Flying Cross (DFC). He was offered a two-year extension in the RAF, but with no guarantee of work thereafter, he left and returned to his pre-war job in insurance. He also returned to the track and his beloved Belgrave Harriers and with the London Olympics in 1948, he made it his goal to secure a place on the team.

'I had barely trained at all so it was a bit disheartening. My times were very slow to start with, nothing like before the war. I trained hard though and put everything into it and by 1947 and 1948 my times started to drop and I went for the team.'

Eight years after he had originally planned to take to the track in Helsinki, he was picked to represent his country in the 5,000m at the age of 31.

'Being an Olympian then was not like it is today I can tell you. I didn't really have a coach, I did meet with one of the hurdles coaches in a tea shop on The Strand one day but that was it. He said to me "Well you know more about your event than me, so just keep it up". That was it, there was no team of helpers or anything like that.'

The Olympics was seen as an opportunity to drag Britain out of its post-war slump. There was still food, petrol and building material rationing in place so no new facilities were built and there was no fancy athletes' village. Instead the world's best were housed in RAF camps on the outskirts of the capital and it soon became known as the Austerity Games. Nevertheless, it was the first time most nations had been together in peacetime for some years – although Germany and Japan were banned from competing.

And despite the low budget, London wanted to put on a spectacle and the opening ceremony was just that. With the royal family in attendance, the 4,000-plus athletes were paraded around Wembley Stadium with marching bands, flag bearers and all the other trappings of such an event. For once even the British weather behaved with temperatures exceeding 90°F (32°C).

'That is the main thing I can remember, the heat. It was so hot and we were paraded around for about four hours. Standing up, sitting down, going over here, going over there. It was enjoyable at the time, but looking back I shouldn't have been there with my race the following day. These days if an athlete was competing the next day they would be rested, opening ceremony or not.'

Bill had been offered accommodation with the rest of the athletes in Uxbridge, where he had been based when he first joined the RAF in 1939. But he instead chose to remain at home with his family.

'I didn't fancy going back to Uxbridge, but looking at it now, that may be where I missed out. We were still on rations back home, even though I was competing, and I think they must have got special food.'

Even on the day of his race he did not get preferential treatment. Where nowadays athletes would be chauffeured to the venue, Bill had to set aside a good few hours to catch a bus, then a train before getting on the tube and then finally walking to the stadium – with the supporters.

'I remember we were taken to an area around the back where we could warm up; it was nothing like they get today. We were then led out and shown to the start line in front of the crowds.'

Lining up alongside Bill was Emil Zátopek, the Czech long-distance runner who is now regarded as one of the greats. He went on to win a gold and a silver at the London Games followed by three gold medals in Helsinki four years later.

'People always ask me what we spoke about, but I didn't speak to him about anything because he couldn't speak English. He was a fantastic athlete and coming to his prime; I was past it at that point. He had been in the Czech Army and was given time to train and race during the war. For every race he won he was promoted. It wasn't like that for us.'

Suffering from sunstroke from the day before, Bill came eighth with Zátopek winning the heat. Only the top four made the final. His dreams of winning an Olympic medal were over and he made his way home on the tube, train and bus, and the following day he was back at work.

He continued to compete until 1955, winning many more titles and has stayed involved with the sport to this day. As well as becoming a track judge, he was a stadium announcer at the White City Stadium where he gained the nickname 'The Golden Voice of Athletics'. He still remains an active member of the Belgrave Harriers and is the oldest living British Olympian. And despite the war denying him a chance at a gold medal and a world record, Bill is not bitter.

'I didn't really think about it during the war, I had other things to worry about. The war just crept up on us all and things had to be put to one side. But I can't complain, I made it through, unlike so many of the other brave men of Bomber Command.'

BOB MORRELL

TO HELL AND BACK IN THE FAR EAST

Japanese prisoner-of-war veteran, Bob Morrell, likes nothing more than walking along Hove Promenade. But for the former RAF mechanic, the past is never far away. He can be strolling along without a care in the world when suddenly he's back in the Far East. The brutal beatings, malaria, searing heat and death are all around him. For a few seconds the horror of his three and a half years as a prisoner are real and present in the supposed comfort of his home city. At best he will recover after a few seconds and carry on with his day. At worst he blacks out.

'They are terrifying. They generally only last a few seconds, but in those seconds I can see so much. They are real. I'm there, I'm back in the Far East. Part of me knows I'm not because I'm thinking, "grab on to that railing", but I'm there, I'm back there.'

Thousands died at the hands of the Japanese more than seventy years ago, but remarkably Bob survived. Just.

Born in May 1921 in Foundry Street, Brighton, Bob worked odd jobs up until his late teens. But with war on the horizon, he decided to follow in his father's footsteps and join the forces. Now living off Lewes Road, Brighton, he remembers the dilemma he faced as if it were yesterday.

'I had read up on the First World War and there was no way I was going to stand in the trenches and get wet feet, so I decided to join the Royal Navy. I went to their recruitment office at the bottom of West Street, Brighton, but it was closed so I walked back up to Queen's Road as someone told me there was another navy place up there. It turned out it was the Royal Marines. There was this bloody great big recruiting officer and he kept slapping me on the back and saying "Just the man for the Marines my son". I was just thinking to myself "please get me out of here". I could never have been a Marine; they were seriously tough.

'I stepped out of there and I should have turned left, gone down to the Clock Tower and home. But for some reason I turned right and walked up towards the station where I came across the RAF recruitment office. To this day I have no idea why I went that way.'

But it was not the glamour of soaring high above the clouds that enticed Bob into the recruitment office that day. It was something altogether a lot simpler.

'I can picture it now; they had an RAF menu for the week in the window. For breakfast there was porridge, bacon, eggs, tea, bread and marmalade. For lunch there was roast beef and Yorkshire pudding, soup, plum duff and custard, then kidneys on toast for tea and a big pint pot of cocoa for supper with slabs of bread pudding. You've got to remember I grew up in the 1920s and 1930s when times were hard, so this was like living in the land of the plenty. They had me with the menu, so I signed up.'

It was September 1938 and Bob was just 17. Training followed and in autumn 1939 he found himself working as a mechanic with No.1 Squadron based at RAF Tangmere, near Chichester. War was declared on Sunday, 3 September, and on the Monday he was on his way to France, travelling by ship from Southampton to Le Havre. One of the most deadly conflicts of all time had just begun, but Bob and the rest of the squadron's support crew were delayed at the port as civilians were using the ferry to go on their holidays.

When they finally arrived in mainland Europe, they made their way to the Belgian border and set up at an airbase from where they launched regular scouting flights towards the French defensive position, the Maginot Line. After just a few weeks they were on the move again, this time to Neuville-sur-Ornain, 60 miles south-east of Reims, where they would spend the next six months. But despite their proximity to the front line, those early months of the war were quiet and there was time for the men to occasionally let their hair down.

'We would get stood down about once every ten days and we would go into the nearby town, Bar-Le-Duc. We used to go to this restaurant and they served these huge platters of horse steak garnished with chops, bacon, eggs, the lot. We got that down us and then we went out on the town. Because I knew a bit of schoolboy French I used to do the translating for the lads and the French girls, so I got lots of drinks bought for me. I remember after one particular night I couldn't go near alcohol for three or four weeks, I was in a hell of a state. But that was how it was, you had to make the most of your time off because you didn't know what was coming up.'

By spring 1940, Hitler was pushing further west and the time for nights out was over with the Battle of France about to begin. By May 'all hell was let loose' Bob remembers, with the ground crews working day and night to keep the squadron in the sky. The pilots took on the Luftwaffe in deadly dogfights in a bid for air supremacy, while Bob and the rest of the ground crews were bombed on a near daily basis. After six months at Neuville-sur-Ornain, the threat of being overrun became too great and the order was given to withdraw. The British Army was sent to Dunkirk, but with Bob and the squadron further south, they were cut off, and instead were forced to make their way west across France.

'People say the French didn't fight and that they just gave up, but they did fight and we were supporting them all the way. We got pushed right across the country and the Germans repeatedly bombed our position. We had to take cover where we could and I tried to fire back with my Lewis gun, but there wasn't much we could do. It was a difficult time.

'I always felt better when I was behind the gun rather than ducking in a trench, hoping for the best. It was luck really whether you got hit or not but I always felt calmer for some reason.'

It was during this deadly game of cat and mouse across France that Bob was very nearly blown to pieces.

'We were under attack from the air and I remember ducking for cover. I heard this terrific whine, then a deafening whistle before a huge thud as a shell hit the ground about 6ft away from me. I waited for the explosion, but there was nothing. I looked up and there it was sticking out the ground, completely intact. I couldn't believe it.'

They continued to move west before reaching Nantes, just 30 miles from the Atlantic and more than 350 miles from Dunkirk. The squadron's Hurricanes had flown back to England but the ground crew was left stranded with the Germans closing in on them. They called for air evacuation and with the enemy literally just up the road, a stripped out Wellington circled before landing to take them home. He had been within minutes of spending his war as a German prisoner.

With a fighter escort, the Wellington made its way back to England and landed at Boscombe Down, Wiltshire. The Battle of France was over; the Battle of Britain was about to begin. By summer 1940, Hitler controlled most of Western Europe and now set his sights on Britain. So confident were the German people of their impending victory that street decorations were put up all over the country.

However, Churchill had other ideas. He rallied the public with his rousing speeches and all available resources were sent to the South of England. The RAF was outnumbered by the Luftwaffe, but they had superior aircraft, in particular the Spitfire and Hurricane. For Bob, it was the latter that was decisive.

'Everyone says that the Spitfire won the Battle of Britain, but it was the Hurricane. They were easier and quicker to make so there were far more of them and they were also much easier to repair and get back in the skies. This was because the Hurricane was largely covered in fabric, compared to the Spitfire that was all metal. You can imagine if the Spitfire got a bullet hole it would be a job for a metal worker, tapping it out and putting a patch on and riveting and whatever. With the Hurricane you just needed a bit of fabric, it was that easy.'

Bob was stationed at RAF Northolt, near Uxbridge, and for the three months and three weeks that the Battle of Britain was fought, he worked non-stop repairing his squadron's Hurricanes.

'You were that busy that you didn't think of it like people think about it today. It was just a case of that kite has to be serviceable by the morning and you got it done. It was hard work and we did twenty-three out of twenty-four hours a day to get them back in the skies. But that was our job and we were needed then more than ever to get on with it.'

As a mechanic, Bob was assigned to an aircraft and a pilot who he stuck with throughout. The only reason for changing would be if your pilot was killed – and with the average life expectancy of a Battle of Britain fighter pilot said to be just four weeks[8], that happened all too regularly.

'You felt the loss of your pilot if he was shot down more than anybody else, as he was yours. I was very lucky; I had someone called Flight Lieutenant John Walker who survived and last I heard was a group captain somewhere. But others weren't as fortunate and it was a huge blow to the morale of a squadron to lose a pilot.'

Despite the odds, the RAF defeated the Luftwaffe and secured air supremacy. Through the skill of the young pilots, superior machines, hard work of the ground crews and the development of radar, Hitler had been stopped in his tracks, with his planned invasion thwarted. Addressing the House of Commons in August 1940, Churchill summed up the country's pride in such an incredible and unlikely victory, delivering his now iconic speech. 'Never in the field of human conflict,' he said, 'was so much owed by so many to so few.'

But for Bob there was no time to ponder the magnitude of what he had just been involved in as he was sent for retraining to become a fitter, before being posted to Scotland in September. Based for six months in Carluke, near Motherwell, his job was to tour crash sites across the Scottish Highlands and islands and salvage what parts he could for the war effort.

'I got to travel all over Scotland with that job and it was safe compared to what I had been doing. But then came the call for me to be sent out to the Far East. I was given ten days' embarkation leave and told to go to Wilmslow outside Manchester where there was a holding camp. From there I was sent back up to Glasgow.'

It was 3 June 1941 when Bob sailed out of Glasgow docks on a troop transporter bound for a part of the world he had only before read about in books. It would be another four and a half years before he would see home again.

Unable to risk going through the Mediterranean to access the Suez Canal because of German U-boats, they headed out into the Atlantic before turning south towards Africa. Their first stop was Freetown, Sierra Leone, followed by Cape Town, Bombay, Sri Lanka and then on to Singapore.

'I had never done any travelling like that; it was amazing seeing all these new places. I grew up in the 1930s so if you managed to go over to France for the day on the boat it was something special. But I remember being very relaxed about it all, I was just trying to enjoy myself while I could.'

It was August by the time they arrived in the British colony of Singapore, which was a strategic outpost for the Allies. Japan was yet to enter the war and the British expats living there had no time for the servicemen.

'They would not talk to us, they wouldn't even say hello to us, that was the fellow Brits out there. I think it was probably a class thing, but as soon as the Japanese bombed Pearl Harbour, then they started to speak. It didn't bother us at all to be honest. Servicemen always make the best of a situation and that's what we did.'

But Bob's feet had barely touched dry land in the island city when he was put back on a ship and sent to an airbase near Kuala Lumpur, the capital of Malaysia. As well as being assigned as part of an anti-paratrooper squad, complete with submachine gun and fifty rounds, he was tasked with setting up a maintenance unit which would take apart engines, service them and get them ready for reuse.

'It was a complete mess out there; nobody knew what they were doing from the very highest in command to the lowest. We were set up at this base and we had the only crankshaft grinder for inline aircraft in the Far East. We were supposed to get Hurricanes out there, but they didn't come until it was too bloody late and there were too few of them anyway.'

After the attack on Pearl Harbour on 7 December, which marked Japan's entry into the war, the Imperial Army started to advance with speed through the jungle towards the Allied lines. Such was the lack of communication in the region that Bob and his colleagues at Kuala Lumpur were unaware of their predicament until the Japanese were right on top of them.

'I remember it was Christmas Day and we had been working on an air conditioning plant at the base to try and make it a bit more bearable. A civvy walked up the stairs and brought us a cheese sandwich and a bottle of beer between the four of us. We shared it out and then got back to work on this huge unit, it was probably about the size of a sofa. It was bloody hard work and we had carried it to the top of these marble stairs when this bod came in looking all panicked and said the Japanese were up the road. We just let it go in pure frustration and it smashed all the way down the stairs, we couldn't believe it. We weren't frightened at that point, we were just so frustrated at all that work which had been for nothing.'

They didn't have the men or the guns to fight and with the Japanese bearing down on them, they abandoned the base and made their way back to the apparent safety of Singapore.

'We were scattered all over the place, nobody really knew what was going on, it was ridiculous. But I didn't really have time to be worried. I knew I had a job to do and I think that helped me overcome any fear of getting killed. When you have got a job, you put all your efforts into doing it, it might be the simplest thing but you have to do it.'

Back in Singapore, the British were remarkably calm given the Japanese were advancing at speed. On arrival in the city, Bob was billeted in a dance hall called the Great World. He looked set to stay there until reinforcements arrived, but one night an Australian pilot officer by the name of Paxton grabbed him and a few of the others and smuggled them aboard a river gunboat.

'I remember him urging us to get in, we didn't really know what was going on, we just followed what he said. The next day, 15 September, Singapore fell. He had seen an opportunity and he found this boat and managed to get a few hundred of us out.'

The fall of Singapore is considered one of Britain's greatest and most costly defeats of the war. The generals believed the island city was impregnable, a stronghold for the Empire in the Far East. They thought that if an attack was to come, it would come from the sea and so all defences were built in anticipation of such an assault. No army, it was said, could attack from inland as it was considered impossible to get through the dense jungle. But the Japanese did and with such speed that they never gave the British a chance to regroup.

The garrison at Singapore had been told that the Japanese would be no match for them. They were said to be poor fighters, performing OK against the Chinese, who they had been fighting with in recent years, but no match for the might of the British Army.[9] But after just eight days of fighting, the city was lost, along with Britain's foothold in the region. More than 5,000 troops were killed or wounded, with 80,000-plus taken prisoner. Thousands of those would die in the brutal prisoner-of-war camps across the Far East in the following few years, but for now, Bob was still a free man.

The river gunboat took them to Batavia, now Jakarta, the capital of Indonesia, where they joined up with a group of American soldiers on their way to Australia. Bob and the rest of the RAF boys helped the Americans load up their kit and in return they promised to send help to rescue them. That help never came.

'It was shortly after that we were told everything had gone haywire. We made our way to a place called Tjilatjap, now Cilacap, in the south of the island of Java, Indonesia, but all the ships there had been blown up. We diverted and went over to Tasikmalaya, about 90 miles away, where we assembled on a racecourse. We were told the Dutch had surrendered on 8 March and we were to do the same. I only had my Tommy gun with just fifty rounds and an extra twenty I had pinched off the Americans. There was no question of fighting, it was hopeless.'

The men were resigned to their fate, and having been on the move for days, they found a stable, mucked it out and went to sleep. It would be another thirty-six hours before the Japanese found them – and when they did there was no thought of putting up a fight. More than seventy years on, Bob still remembers the moment he was captured all too clearly.

'You were scared. Any man who said he was not scared was a liar, you just suppressed it. We really didn't know what was going to happen. But if we had known then how we were going to starve, how we were going to be beaten and how we were going to die, I think every one of us would have shot himself instead of being taken prisoner.'

The next three and a half years would change Bob forever, but the first few weeks of life as a prisoner were not all bad. They were taken to Jogjakarta (now Yogyakarta) in the south of Java, and ordered to fill in bomb craters at a nearby airfield where they played tricks on their captors. 'We had our fun with them. We would have to fill in the holes with a mixture of rock and earth and then call in their steamroller. But we would fill in the holes with just the earth and then give them the all-clear to roll over. Of course the roller would fall straight down into the hole and they would be furious.'

But even in those early days, conditions were grim and food was scarce. They lived and slept in the mangled remains of aircraft hangars that the Dutch had bombed and they got by on what little provisions they were given. It was here that the first outbreak of disease hit the group, with mosquitoes carrying malaria and dengue fever into the camp. Dozens succumbed to the illnesses, which were largely treatable if medical help had been made available.

Before long they were on the move again, this time to Surabaya on the north coast of Java, where they were taken out to the docks to move huge twisted girders. It was hard manual labour and many of the men were simply too weak to continue.

'Even in those early months life was hard and you had to take every possible opportunity to get food and other provisions. The only problem was if we were caught. If you were lucky you would get away with a crack around the head but if they had a bamboo stick then you would get whipped. That kind of punishment was a daily thing; any infringement and you would get beaten. This was part of everyday life for us with the Japanese but you had to ride it out and get on with it. The treatment we faced had a devastating effect on many of us and I still get flashbacks of the beatings today.'

They remained in Surabaya for the best part of a year, carrying out the near impossible task of untwisting the tangled girders with little more than their bare hands. But in April 1943, the Japanese promised change and told the prisoners they would be taken to an island where everything would be better for them. That island was called Haruku – sometimes spelt Haroekoe – and it would claim the lives of hundreds.

The 2,000 prisoners deemed fit enough to go were transported in a small cargo ship called the *Amagi Maru*. The weak, malnourished and diseased men boarded the vessel, with the Japanese guards hurrying them along with their bayonets. Once on the filthy, cramped deck they were ushered down into the hold, climbing one by one down the single ladder leading into darkness. Occasionally the impatient guards would shove the men, causing them to tumble down on top of each other. Down in the hold there was little air or light and barely enough room to move.

'It was awful, it was hot, it was claustrophobic and everyone was frightened. There was just one ladder going to the top and the men suffering from dysentery had to queue to make their way up to use just three toilets – for 2,000 sick men.'

Just as the *Amagi Maru* was about to set off on its near three-week voyage, the Americans bombed the harbour and blew up another ship anchored there. The guards went into a frenzy and crammed the remaining prisoners down in the hold before firing up the engines. More than seventy years on, Bob still struggles to talk about what happened next.

'It was panic stations. They came and put the covers on and we were down there in the dark and the only bit of light was the top of that ladder. It was like that for seventeen days. There was no air, no food, no medical supplies; it was awful. I will never forget it.'

Throughout the 1,000 mile-plus journey, prisoners died as dysentery spread. And with just three toilets between the men, the smell on the deck was awful, with many of the prisoners unable to control their bowels. As if the spread of disease was not bad enough, they also had to endure the beatings that were dished out by the guards for the slightest misdemeanour. An example of such an offence could include forgetting to bow to a guard on the way to the toilet. If the prisoner was lucky, his forgetfulness would result in a rifle butt to the face.

After more than two weeks in the cramped, squalid conditions, the ship arrived at the island of Ambon, where those who could swim were ordered to unload bombs, petrol and other supplies. The prisoners, regardless of their swimming ability, put themselves forward for the task, so they could wash themselves in the seawater. But before long they were packed into the hold once more as the captain set course for their final destination.

It had been seventeen days since they left Surabaya and the journey had claimed many lives. But those who had survived were upbeat, convinced the conditions at their new home, Haruku, would be better than those aboard the *Amagi Maru*. How wrong they were.

Around 800 miles west of Papua New Guinea and 600 miles north of the Australian city of Darwin, the small island of Haruku was strategically important for the Japanese. They wanted to build an airstrip there to launch attacks on the north coast of Australia and so Bob and his fellow prisoners were tasked with carving off the peaks of two hills on the islands and constructing a runway over the top.

On arrival nearly all of the men were suffering from dysentery and to make matters worse, it was monsoon season. The heavy rains had all but washed away the huts the natives had built for them, leaving the prisoners at the mercy of the elements.

'I remember us landing and it was absolutely pouring. We just lay there shattered in the rain and god knows what else. The few latrines that we did have flooded before long, which only led to more disease around the camp. There was nowhere for us to sleep because the huts were pretty much destroyed, I'd never experienced weather like it before.'

The camp was crawling with maggots and lice and the men were rationed small portions of rice and little else. But they were not just expected to survive in the conditions; they also had to work.

'The men were so weak and the work so punishing that many simply collapsed and died. We were working on coral and we were chipping away at it with 6in chisels and a hammer. It was no good and we were all already ill and weak from a lack of food.

'They didn't see us as human beings; we were slaves. To this day I just don't understand their mentality. If they wanted the job done, they could have treated us well, fed us, looked after us and we would have done it well and done it quick. But they didn't, we worked dawn until dusk, with little food, no medicine and they beat us and beat us and beat us. I will never understand and I will never forgive them.'

Of the 2,000 men that made the journey over to the island, around 600 died during the eighteen months they were there. The prisoners were buried on a plot close to camp and initially the men were given coffins made from a few planks. But as the body count began to rise, they had to craft their own makeshift caskets from green bamboo. As one of the fitter prisoners, it was often down to Bob to carry the coffins to the burial site.

'When I came back from a day's work, they would look at me and gesture at the bodies. That was one of the problems of being one of the so-called fit ones. I would have to carry the coffins over to the pit. I just wanted to collapse and sleep, but I had to carry ten, sometimes twelve, coffins at the end of a long day. It's hard to think of now but war does funny things to your mind. I resented them dying. I thought to myself "I've had enough and now I've got to carry you over there". It's not "poor old Bill", it's "why did he have to bloody die on my bloody shift".'

The near daily funeral procession reduced those left alive to physical and mental wrecks, as they were forced to march through the unceasing rain in near darkness, carrying their former campmates. Usually led by an officer who would light a candle to guide the way, guards would be at the rear with bayonets fixed in case anyone tried to escape. If they were lucky, a grave would have been dug for them. If not, they would have to claw away at the coral using their hands. There was little room for respect and dignity on the island – even for the dead – and at the height of the dysentery epidemic, it was not unusual for a dozen or more men to be buried in the same grave.

The guards cared little for what happened to them and one in particular made life unbearable for the prisoners. He was a sergeant called Gunso Mori – a veteran of the Chinese war who is believed to have contracted syphilis during the rape and conquest of the country. It was rumoured that the war and subsequent disease drove him insane and he dished out brutal daily beatings to prisoners who were too weak and ill to defend themselves.[10] Whether he used his parade baton, a bamboo stick or his belt, he would beat the prisoners to within an inch of their lives. This practice was usually carried out on the parade ground so the other prisoners could see and, as a result of the public beatings, his junior officers also adopted a more callous and violent attitude.

But while his violence pushed the men to the brink, Mori's greatest crime was refusing to allow the prisoners to build a latrine over the sea as he said it would 'sully the ocean belonging to His Imperial Emperor'.[11] Instead excrement over-flowed from the hastily dug pits near camp, which brought flies and maggots, spread disease and led to hundreds of deaths. Mori was captured following the Japanese surrender and executed for multiple war crimes in Singapore.

Bob had spent more than eighteen months on Haruku when, in autumn 1944, the Americans began to bomb the island.

'At times they had more than 100 planes and they would attack the docks. We weren't allowed to take cover, we just had to sit there and hope they didn't hit us. All I can say is thank goodness they were Yanks, because they never hit the bloody target. They literally cleared the town and goodness knows what else but they completely missed the docks.'

By September, the Americans were advancing west through Papua New Guinea and the order was given to move the prisoners back to Ambon and then to Surabaya.

The men were loaded on to a transport ship called the *Maros Maru*, and if they thought their journey to the island had been horrific, it was nothing compared to what they were about to experience. Determined not to leave anyone behind to be rescued by the Americans, all the men, regardless of their condition, were loaded on to the 600-tonne vessel. The ship was barely seaworthy, having been sunk off Jakarta in 1942 only to be refloated again by the Japanese the following year for prisoner transportation. There were few facilities on board and the 630 men, some collected from surrounding islands, were packed into every conceiv-able space for the hellish journey. Those who were lucky were squeezed below deck with scarcely enough air to survive and next to no light. The unlucky ones were forced to stand on deck to burn in the tropical sun. Men collapsed from dehydration and heat stroke as the sun literally cooked them, leaving their bodies covered in huge sores and blisters. The British officers pleaded with the guards to provide shade for the dying men, but it was not until thirty had succumbed to the heat that an awning was erected.

Food and water were again at a minimum and the prisoners were given less than half a pint to drink each day. Not that there was any shortage, as the guards bathed in huge drums of drinking water in front of the men to compound their misery.

One prisoner, so delirious and weak from dehydration and disease, went to climb over the ship's rail to use the latrine box and fell overboard. He was quickly rescued, but the British officers were lined up and lashed for not keeping him under control. Sergeant Mori was also aboard and he continued his reign of terror. An RAF officer by the name of Flight Lieutenant W. Blackwood gave an account at the Japanese war trials of one incident involving Mori on the *Maros Maru*:

'One night, as a sick Dutchman lay dying, he began hiccoughing loudly at regular intervals, Sergeant Mori appeared on the bridge and threatened to beat all the sick unless the dying man was given an injection to keep him quiet. This was done but within half an hour he was awake again and hiccoughing as before. Sergeant Mori repeated his threat and another injection was given. Yet a third time the hiccoughing started. The Japanese sergeant came back on to the bridge and, yelling at the top of his voice, threatened to come down and lay about him with a stick among the stretcher cases. A third injection was given but the Dutchman was never heard again for he died.'[12]

Weeks passed and the death toll continued to rise as the men succumbed to starvation, dehydration and disease. Those who died were thrown overboard with a sandbag tied to their leg. If the guards allowed, friends would conduct a simple funeral service for them before they went over the side. For those left alive, it was almost too much to bear as Flight Lieutenant Blackwood explained at the war trials:

'All the men lay spread out on the uneven bundles of firewood blistering horribly in the tropical sun. Tongues began to blacken, raw shirtless shoulders began to bleed and all vestige of sanity deserted many. The night air was filled with the yells and screams of the dying, the curses of the worn-out trying to get some sleep, and the chronic hiccoughing that afflicts a man about to die of beriberi.'[13]

After a couple of weeks at sea the *Maros Maru* came to a juddering halt. The engines had packed in and, as the Japanese crew lacked any technical knowledge, they appealed to the prisoners, many of whom were Royal Navy or RAF engineers, for help.

After being temporarily patched up, the ship diverted to Makassar, a small port city in South Sulawesi, Indonesia. But much to the confusion of the men, she remained anchored and they were not allowed to get off. For days on end there was no movement and the men were forced to try and survive on what food and water they still had. It was forty days before the engines were fired up once more and they got moving. In that time another 150 had died.

Back at sea, the spread of disease worsened and more men perished. One account given at the Japanese war trials describes how a young prisoner, delirious with sunstroke, continually screamed and shouted the thoughts of his disordered mind for nearly thirty hours until he became too weak to speak. Then, just before his body and mind gave in, he grabbed a full tin, which had been used as a bedpan, and drank the lot thinking it was water. He died shortly afterwards.[14]

Just like the young prisoner, Bob's body and mind were deteriorating day by day. And with their destination still a long way off, he came to accept that he too would die and, with a sandbag tied to his leg, sink to the bottom of the sea.

'It was the only time I gave up. I was sick and I knew that I probably had just a few hours before I was over the side. But then I heard someone call out "You're from Brighton aren't you?" It was a man called Pat Hunt, I had no idea how he knew me or knew I was from Brighton. Maybe I was delirious and was saying something about home. Anyway, he got me up on the hatch after someone was thrown over the side and lay me down next to this Dutchman who was on the way out. We waited because we knew in his haversack he had some tobacco and when he died we smoked it. That kept me going. Sometimes it is the smallest thing you grab on to and that's why I'm here today.'

After sixty-seven hellish days at sea, the *Maros Maru* finally arrived at Surabaya. Of the 630 men who had departed, just 325 were left. Those still alive were shells of their former selves. Half-starved, beaten and delirious from the heat, they helped each other on to the quayside. Bob was barely conscious and had to be carried from the ship by his friends.

'I had lost all movement in my hands and legs. I will always remember lying there on the quayside at Surabaya and one of our gang, Derek, got this deep mess tin of water and kept pouring it over me to cool me down. My body was so dehydrated and that kind act just eased the suffering ever so slightly.

'I was then loaded on to a train and taken to Batavia (Jakarta) where the Japanese had allowed us to set up a hospital in an old school. I don't know why they did, I guess one of them got soft hearted or something.'

Bob drifted in and out of consciousness as he was transported across Java. On arrival at the hospital he was stripped, shaved from head to toe – to get rid of the lice – and then hosed down. At that point he passed out.

'The next thing I remember I came to and I was laying in a bed, in a cool, clean hospital ward. I remember thinking "I'm in heaven". Luckily the doctors had just had a shipment of vitamin B2 and so they could start treating me straightaway. The staff were overwhelmed so us men had to help each other out. If my hands weren't working then I would get my mate in the bed next to me to feed me and if his legs were dead then I would rub them for him to bring them back to life.'

The men were suffering from all sorts of diseases, but mostly it was beriberi, an illness common among prisoners surviving on just rice. Those with the disease filled with fluid from the feet up, an affliction that would slowly paralyse them. Any physical contact was agonisingly painful until the heart eventually gave in under the strain.

For months Bob tried to summon the strength to get out of his bed, but he was just too weak. On good days he could cling on to the bedposts and pull himself around, but walking unaided was too much for his battered body. But help came from a fellow Brightonian called Reg Penny, who was in the same hospital.

'He was a bit better than me and he used to come downstairs to where I was to bring me a cigarette. Every day he would come and we would have a smoke and a chat. Then one day he stopped coming down and told me I would have to come up to him if I wanted a smoke. So I got on my hands and knees and crawled over to the stairs and shuffled my way up to him. That was what got me going and got me moving again.

'I felt like I was in between life and death in that hospital, especially at the start. It is difficult to explain but I wasn't sure where I was, all I know is that I had the will to survive, I wasn't giving up.'

During Bob's six months in the hospital, he also experienced his first flashback. But rather than taking him back to the horrors of Haruku or the *Maros Maru*, they were flashbacks of home. While sitting in his bed waiting to be seen by the doctor, his mind would take him back to England and he would be in his front room in Brighton, waiting for his mum to bring him a cup of tea. The doctors did not know what to say or do, and so as soon as he was on his feet again, Bob was discharged and sent to a prisoner-of-war camp near Jakarta. Apart from a short spell at a camp at Bandong, 100 miles south-east of the capital, Bob remained there for the rest of his days as a captive. It was during his time at Bandong the Americans brought about the beginning of the end of the war.

'I remember we would queue up at meal times and we would get a bowl of rice. Then one day, out of nowhere, we had meat. An ox had been killed and had been brought into camp. I remember thinking that the war must be over. Shortly after we got moved back to Batavia (Jakarta) and I tried to talk to one of the nicer guards in the hope of getting a cigarette or anything to be honest. But all I could get from him was that he was saying something about a huge explosion in Japan.'

That explosion was, of course, the first atomic bomb dropped on Hiroshima in the south of the country on 6 August 1945. The *Enola Gay*, an American Boeing B-29 Superfortress, named after the mother of the pilot, dropped the bomb code-named Little Boy on the key industrial and military city, killing between 90,000 and 166,000 people. Just days later, on 9 August, the industrial city of Nagasaki was targeted with a plutonium bomb codenamed Fat Man. Half the city was destroyed and between 39,000 and 80,000 people were killed. The intention had been to scare the enemy and avoid a full-scale invasion of Japan, which it was estimated would result in more than 1 million dead. It worked, and just six days after the second bomb was dropped, Japan announced its surrender.

When Bob and his fellow prisoners arrived back at the camp in Jakarta, the Japanese soon started to disappear. What they had dreamt of for three and a half years was finally confirmed when two Allied majors parachuted in to tell them the war was over and they were free men.

'I remember they said, "For goodness sake, don't do anything because there are bugger all supplies here". We didn't have any troops and for the first few days there was no extra food or anything. When the British finally arrived, supplies did start coming through though and I volunteered to help out at the nearby aerodrome where they parachuted all the stuff in. We used to get first pick so we ate the best and we smoked the best before dishing it out to everyone else.

'There were mixed feelings for me: on one hand I was delighted that it was all over and we finally had food. It may sound silly but when you are just trying to survive, food is such a major thing. For three and a half years that is all we did, we looked for food and now we could have anything we wanted. But I was also thinking of all the men we had lost. It was all about survival those years, I didn't have time to mourn those who had died, it was just day-to-day, grabbing on to the next thing and getting through it.

'You talk to other men and they can't tell you why they survived, they only know that they did survive and that's the same with me. When you face death on a daily basis you soon find out if you have the will to live.'

Despite the defeat of the Japanese, Bob and his fellow prisoners were not out of danger. The Dutch, who once held Java as one of their colonies, were determined to have it back. In their way stood a man named Sukarno, later to become the first president of Indonesia, who was leading his country's fight for independence. To one of Sukarno's men, Bob and the other prisoners of war looked like Dutchmen and so they had to tread carefully while waiting to be taken home.

But finally, after more than four years in the Far East, the order came through for Bob to board a flight across the United States and back to Europe. He was all set to be reunited with his family when an American general decided that he wanted to use the plane.

Bob and his fellow prisoners were instead taken back to Singapore, the city he had escaped in February 1942, before boarding a ship which took them to Sri Lanka, then to Bombay and up through the Suez Canal and into the Mediterranean.

'As we were getting closer to Liverpool, me and my mate George went for a sleep. The next thing we knew we were the only ones left on the ship. We were that exhausted that we had missed the big welcome and were all alone. A flight lieutenant found us and wanted to know who the hell we were. He ushered us off and gave us a cup of tea and cigarettes before a group captain collected us and told us we were to report to RAF Cosford in Shropshire. We travelled in style and were chauffeured in this big fancy car by the flight lieutenant. I remember we turned to him and asked if we could stop at a pub. He refused, but he bought us a couple of ice creams instead.'

At RAF Cosford the men were only allowed to go home once they had passed the required medical tests. The problem was, with everyone heading to the mess and catching up on the beer they had missed out on over the last four years, they almost all failed their samples the following morning. But after a couple of nights off, Bob was given the all-clear to return to Brighton and was taken to the station at Wolverhampton to be put on a train to London. On reaching the capital, transport was put on to take him to Victoria, where he got the service down to the coast.

When he pulled into his hometown in early November 1945, it was a city largely unchanged. But for Bob the last three and a half years had changed him deeply.

'I remember arriving at the station and seeing my mother and father. We went back to Brunswick Mews, where we were living, and everybody was there and happy to see me. Cecil and Hetty Bennett, who ran the Brunswick pub, had even organised a party for me.

'I felt like I should have been screaming my head off with joy, but it just got too much at times. I just wanted to be at home, I just wanted to get back to normal.'

Bob left the RAF not long after the war. But his experiences during those few years never left him. Even now, more than seventy years on, those memories stay close in the form of terrifying flashbacks.

'There is no rhyme or reason to them; they just come out of the blue when I least expect them. I can be walking along without a care in the world when they hit me. Thankfully I always seem to be near a railing or a bench so I can sit down or hang on and get through it. They generally only last a matter of seconds, but they are very real and very frightening. When I get them I'm there, I'm back there in the Far East.'

When Bob retired the flashbacks began to get worse and when his wife, Sylvia, died in 1998, he was at a loss as to what to do.

'I can't remember who said it, but one day someone mentioned getting in touch with Combat Stress. All I can say to that person is thank you, because they saved me. I cannot say enough good things about Combat Stress; they enabled me to talk about my time during the war for the first time. They encouraged me not to bottle it all up and that's why I can tell you my story today.'

Combat Stress is a veterans' mental health charity based in Leatherhead, Surrey. And as the name suggests, their support workers help veterans of all ages suffering from combat stress that can result in depression, flashbacks, insomnia and nightmares.

'They were a real lifeline for me, along with the Java Far East Prisoners of War Club. I would recommend them to anyone of any age who is suffering.

'I still get the flashbacks and I imagine I will always have them, but I can deal with them now. The truth is my experiences during the war will never leave me.'

Arthur Ayres in uniform; on his wedding day with his wife Louisa; and at his home in Portslade in 2014. (© *The Argus*/Simon Dack)

Bill Lucas DFC with his medals at home in Cowfold in 2015; and looking at his flight log, which details his eighty-one wartime sorties and shows his participation in the 1,000 bomber raid on Cologne. (© Ben James)

Bob Morrell in uniform in September 1939; and at his home in Brighton in 2015.
(© *The Argus*/Terry Applin)

Shindy Perez (middle row, third from the left) with her school class before the war; just three of those pictured survived the concentration camps. Also pictured at her home in Hove in 2015. (© Shindy Perez and *The Argus*/Terry Applin)

John Buckeridge at his home in Cuckfield in 2015. (© Ben James)

Jack Lyon pictured at his Bexhill home in 2014. (© *The Argus*/Liz Finlayson)

NO. 1 AIR OBSERVER'S COURSE.

STANDING:- L.A.C.'s HOLMES. HARPER. LAKIN. KEMP. KNIGHT.

SITTING:- L.A.C.'s LYON. HATTON. LAWSON. GEOGHEGAN. HOBSON.

Top: Jack Lyon (front row, far left) while on the No. 1 Air Observer's course prior to being shot down. Bottom: a newspaper cutting shows Jack (front row, right) in one of Stalag Luft III's huts prior to the escape attempt. (© Jack Lyon)

Patrick Delaforce (top: front row, far right) relaxing with other officers in Holland in March 1945; and again (bottom: on the right) standing in front of the Sexton 26-pounder guns on 10 May 1945. (© Patrick Delaforce)

A burning Mark IV Panzer tank near Argentan, Normandy, during Operation Bluecoat, July/August 1944. (© Patrick Delaforce)

German armour destroyed by the 11th Armoured Division in Normandy in June 1944; and the 11th Armoured Division accompanied by infantry units on their way through Nazi-occupied Europe. (© Patrick Delaforce)

Top: Patrick Delaforce (middle foreground) presiding over the trial of Willi Erold and eleven others at the Oldenburg War Crimes Tribunal in September 1946. Erold and six others were sentenced to death by hanging. Bottom: Patrick at his home in Brighton in front of a family portrait. (© Patrick Delaforce)

Maurice Macey pictured at his Westham home with the cooking pan he credits with saving his life. Opposite page: Maurice in his uniform and stood on the left with his good friend Peter Clarke. Lastly, his flight log, showing his sorties on D-Day, with the caption 'quite a day, bags of action'. (© Ben James and Maurice Macey)

(1)	(2)	(3)	(4)			(5)	(6)	(7)	(8)	(9)	(10)	(11)	(12)	(13)
	·25				Johnnie Pearson his on shipping Recco. missing.									
	23·10				D. Hillwood F/LT O/C FLIGHT									
					C.F. Hadley S/LDR O/C 124 SQD.									
	·45													
	·35													
1·10	1·10				one ship burning in convoy eventually abandoned.						·20			
1·35	1·35		}	"D.DAY.	→ quite a day, bags of action									
1·40	·40		}											
1·35	1·25		}											
1·20	1·30				$\frac{10}{10}$ cloud all the day 'dead loss'						1·00			
1·00	1·00													
1·35	1·35				bags of gliders & coloured chut in the field.									
					Navy very touchy									
18·0	116·45	208·40	11·05	9·60								23·05	14·35	14·40

Above: John Akehurst in his uniform, *c.* 1939. Opposite page: John in his flying suit, *c.* 1940, and in later life with his medals at his house in Peacehaven. His flight log shows his final mission, with the entry 'Opperations [*sic*] Bremen. Failed to return.' (© *The Argus*/Tony Wood and Ben James)

To   WITNEY o. RETURN   1.40

FROM   BASSINGBOURNE   & AIR TEST   .30

OPPERATIONS   BREMEN
   Failed to Return.

                                                  S/LD

                                                  o/c B

- FORTRESS -
RLREED LA

From John Akehurst's prisoner-of-war notebook: a drawing of an American bomber and German fighter, as well as a self-portrait with a list of all the camps he was confined in. (© Ben James)

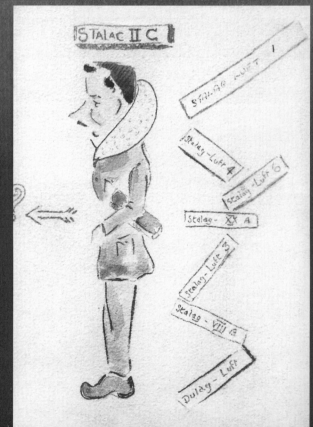

SHINDY PEREZ

SURVING AUSCHWITZ'S GAS CHAMBERS

S ixteen-year-old Shindy Perez had just arrived at the gates of Auschwitz when an SS officer ordered the prisoners into two columns. She clung on to her grandmother, who held her close. But with the two lines moving forward, she pushed Shindy into the other queue, and lied to the guard about the frail teenager's age. Minutes later Shindy had lost sight of her and was stripped and shaved from head to toe before being marched into the shower block. Scared and confused, she looked up at the taps and waited. Minutes passed but nothing happened and she was ushered out by the guards. She desperately searched for her grandmother, expecting to find her on the other side. But she never saw her again.

Born in the small town of Vylok, now in western Ukraine, Shindy was raised by her grandparents. Her father died before she was born and her mother was rarely around to look after her. It was her grandmother, Fani, and grandfather, Sandor Alexander, who she thought of as her parents.

The couple had children later in life who grew up alongside Shindy. Although aunts, Margit, the same age as Shindy, and Aranka, two years older, were more like sisters and their close bond would keep the trio alive through what was to come.

Life was hard for the family in the 1920s and 1930s, but they were happy. They lived off a small dairy herd and would rise at 5 a.m. each morning to milk the cows. For Shindy, it was school she really loved, and in particular her teacher, who instilled in her a passion for learning.

Now in her late eighties and living in Hove, she remembers him well. 'He was nice to me and my aunt, he used to like the Jewish kids in the class because we were clever. But he was fond of us all really. We had a bit of a garden and he taught us to propagate rose bushes and other things. In the summer time when school closed we used to go and feed the silk worms with mulberry leaves with him. He was quite advanced for the time as a teacher.'

But like most others, he too got caught up in Hitler's drive to conquer. He was called up to the Hungarian Army – who were fighting alongside the Nazis – and killed in action.

'I was looking at a school photograph I still have just the other day. He picked about fifteen children to be in the picture and of those fifteen, who were mostly Jews, just myself, my aunt and another Jewish boy, Zrilu, survived the war.'

The photograph typifies the devastation Jewish communities across Europe experienced with Hitler's rise. And the story of Zrilu hammers home the heart-breaking reality of the numbers attached to Hitler's Final Solution.

Zrilu was top of the class. His best friend was an equally bright girl at the same school called Lilly Schreiber. She was a pretty girl with blond, gingery hair and freckles. With German troops bearing down on the town the two young teenagers made a pact. After it was all over they would return to Vylok and be reunited.

Zrilu survived the war and returned as planned to the town to try and rebuild his life. He went to the station and waited for the two daily services – one in the morning and one at night. But there was no sign of Lilly. So the following day he got up and went down to meet the morning train again. But there was still no sign of her. He did the same again in the evening, with the same result. He con-tinued this for the next week and then the week after that and the week after that. For another six months, Zrilu waited at the station, meeting the morning and evening train, hoping to see Lilly walk down the platform. But she had been killed, another victim of the concentration camps.

For Shindy and the people of Vylok, life changed in 1938 when the Hungarian Army invaded. The region had been under Hungarian rule prior to the First World War, later to be taken by Czechoslovakia. But with the backing of the German Army, Hungary saw an opportunity to recapture the region.

Shindy was just 10 years old when the troops moved in and life changed over-night – especially for the Jewish population. Their stores and businesses were closed, men were forced into slave labour and random acts of violence and killings became common. Most people were allowed to stay in their own homes and Shindy and her friends remained at school. But anti-Semitism was rife and they were left under no illusion about who was in charge. Meanwhile Shindy's mother had left for England, seeking refuge with her two brothers. Shindy's grandmother tried to persuade her and her aunts to escape, but they refused to leave her side.

'I remember that they took away the men and forced them to work in the forest and on the railway. People couldn't afford to live any more because they closed down all the shops, we would have to get by on whatever we could or we would have to sell on the quiet. We had a curfew as well and we could not go out after 6 p.m., they completely controlled us. Worst of all the Hungarian soldiers would randomly pick Jewish boys and take them to the forest and shoot them, there was nothing we could do. Anti-Semitism was rampant.'

This continued for six years until 1944. But as bad as life may have seemed, it was nothing compared to what was to come. Hitler had become impatient and wanted control of the region and so sent in his troops. He then ordered Adolf Eichmann, widely regarded as the architect of the Holocaust, to round up the Jewish population.

'It was April 1944 when they came. I remember they went round the town with the Hungarian soldiers; they came to our houses and took whatever they wanted. Within ten minutes everything was gone.'

The Jewish people of Vylok were ordered to march to the next town with whatever they could carry. After some 25 miles they arrived at what would be their new home for the next few weeks.

'It was a ghetto, conditions were terrible, there was little shelter, no sanitation and no cooking facilities. My grandmother got two bricks and a pan and would cook whatever she could find. I was really concerned about my grandfather though who was getting ill, he was 70 at the time so it was especially difficult for him. But we had no option, we couldn't go anywhere and there was nobody to help us.'

For a month the family lived in squalid conditions at the mercy of the weather. That was until the order was given for them to board a train for Poland – their destination was Auschwitz.

'We knew nothing of Auschwitz or the concentration camps; we had no idea. We didn't know where we were going, we just knew that we had to get on this train in these wagons.

'The journey was awful; there must have been sixty or seventy people to a wagon. There was no water, no food, no sanitation, no nothing. If you found a little hole in the cracks you would go to the toilet there, but that was it. They treated us like animals; the soldiers would pull my granddad by his beard, so it was cut off. He cried afterwards, he was unrecognisable.'

The journey to southern Poland would take them a couple of days, during which they passed through Shindy's hometown. By the time they arrived at the death camp it was the end of May 1944. Exhausted and starving, they pulled into the station with the now infamous concentration camp gates ahead of them.

Thousands of weak and emaciated bodies poured out of the wagons and began to line up outside of what they assumed would be some sort of working camp. Barbed wire surrounded the perimeter and all they could see were a series of barracks and huge chimneys pumping out smoke.

'We were ushered out of the wagons but my grandfather forgot his prayer book and shawl. He asked a guard if he could go back and get it and the guard said "You don't need it, there are plenty more in there". I remember I was holding my grandmother's hand and my two aunts were with me.

'We were then separated into two lines: men and women. It all happened in a second, I didn't get a chance to say goodbye to my grandfather. I thought I would see him inside.'

As the four women – Shindy, her grandmother and two aunts – moved further forward in the queue, they came across a group of SS officers keeping a close eye over proceedings. One slim, tall man appeared to be of particular importance. Shindy would later come to recognise him as Adolf Eichmann. As a lieutenant colonel of the SS, he was placed in charge of the logistics for transporting millions of Jews from ghettos around Europe to the death camps. His most efficient and deadly camp was Auschwitz. It is estimated that under his command between 5.5 million and 6 million Jews were killed during the Second World War. Such was his crazed determination that towards the end he proclaimed, 'I will leap into my grave laughing, because the fact that I have the death of 5 million Jews on my conscience gives me extraordinary satisfaction'.[15]

But back in the queues outside Auschwitz, Shindy had no idea what lay ahead, nor did she know the type of man she was standing just yards from. Another order was given to form two lines: one for 18 to 45 year olds and another for all those younger and older. Still clenching her grandmother's hand, 16-year-old Shindy went to join the second line.

But sensing what was ahead – seeing the weak and frail grouped together – her grandmother shoved the teenage girls towards the other line and told the SS guard they were all 18. Shindy tried to run back but she was pushed into the line again by her grandmother.

'I didn't get the chance to say anything to her, it all happened in seconds. She went off in her queue and we were in ours. I thought I would see her inside. When we got past the gate I remember asking someone who had been in Auschwitz for some time when we would see them again. They replied, "See them? What are you talking about, can you not see those chimneys up there?" But we didn't believe it.'

The SS considered those aged 18 to 45 useful as a means of slave labour and spared them. Anyone younger or older would be sent to the gas chambers. Her grandmother's quick thinking had saved the three youngsters.

Once inside the camp, guards took the girls' details and they were given a number. They were then stripped and made to stand for hours, naked, until someone came and shaved them from head to toe.

'They shaved every part of our body, our heads, arm pits, private parts. They were rough though and when they cut the skin they would pour petrol on it so you were stinging from head to toe. All we wanted to do at that point was to get in a shower and wash whatever it was off.'

As if on a production line, the prisoners were next ushered into what appeared to be a shower block. But no water came out of these taps; the plumbing was instead rigged to spray hydrogen cyanide. The three stood and waited for the showers to come on, but there was nothing. They were sent through the other side and each handed a single dress before being told to await their next orders.

'Husbands and wives didn't recognise each other; everyone had been shaved all over. I remember we were then taken to a toilet block and that was where we were told to stay. You were lucky if you could sleep on the wooden seat, but otherwise you would be on the concrete floor. There was no food or drinking water and we were so thirsty we used to stand at the side of the roof and hold our hands out to try and catch the rainwater. It was horrendous.'

Those who did survive the shower block usually remained in Auschwitz for just a matter of days before being transferred to a working camp. But for many, especially those who had been separated from family and friends, it all became too much. One way out was to run at the electric fence surrounding the perimeter, a horrific decision Shindy witnessed many take. But for her, she still had her two aunts, Margit and Aranka, and the three of them stuck together.

'It is difficult to explain how we got through it, especially to someone who wasn't there. My brain just blocked it all out, I didn't really think of anything. I wasn't thinking about my grandparents or escaping or the end of the war. I just shut off from everything; I was like a zombie. I think the brain must protect you like that. I forgot everything.'

After two weeks in Auschwitz, the three girls were transported north towards Tallinn. Crammed into wagons like cattle, it was the best part of a day before they arrived at an old brick factory just outside the Estonian capital. There they were put to work, twelve hours a day, seven days a week. They received little food and tried to rest in lice-infested sleeping quarters.

'In the morning we were given a cup of ersatz coffee (a coffee substitute) but no food. Then at lunch we got mushroom soup. They called it that but really it was just water with worms – which had been in the mushroom stalks – floating on the top. We used to chuck it but the Russian prisoners, who were in the same camp, were so hungry that they would eat it. Then at night after work we would get one thin slice of bread. We were all so thin, our hips stuck out and there was a big hole in the middle. We were empty.'

Despite the lack of food, they were expected to work twelve hours each day, usually carrying out backbreaking work. And when they were not at work they would try to sleep in their cramped, filthy and bug-ridden rooms.

'It was five to a bunk and the lice were rampant. The guards would often wake us up at three in the morning and you were pleased to get up because the lice would be eating you, it was terrible. But we never thought about escaping. They would bring those who had tried to escape back into camp, they were black and blue and they would dump them on the floor to show you what would happen if you tried anything.'

One of Shindy's jobs at the camp was to help a local workman mix cement in a large bathtub. It was a job for a strong man, not a malnourished teenage girl. Yet during those dark days of slave labour, Shindy still glimpsed some signs of humanity. One day, when her body was close to giving up, a Russian prisoner who was also assigned to the workman, saw Shindy struggling. Although the two did not share a language, he let her know that he would take over so she could rest. He then measured Shindy's finger and later returned with a brass ring that he had made with her initials carved into the central section. Shortly after he was reassigned to a different job and she never saw the Russian again. Prisoners were strictly prohibited from keeping personal possessions and she hid the ring from the guards.

Shindy too was soon reassigned, this time ordered to empty big stones from wagons destined for the brick factory. The work, lack of food and sleep were beginning to take their toll. Her mind continued to do its best to shut out the horrors as the prisoners were exposed to the same brutal and exhausting daily schedule. As while the weak died or were shot, the stronger ones had to continue.

But with the Russians edging ever closer to Berlin, the order was given to move the prisoners further west. They were called outside on to the parade ground and lined up for inspection. Only those deemed fit and healthy enough would travel. For those too weak, graves had already been prepared. At these inspections, Shindy did everything she could to survive.

'I stood, like I did at every selection, next to my friend from the camp. The poor girl was white and pale and much skinnier than me. If I stood on my toes, I looked bigger and if I put my chest out I could look strong. They took her away and I was put on a boat with my aunts and we sailed from Tallinn.'

Hundreds were crammed on to the boat with no access to toilets, food or water. For two days and nights they were trapped down below deck as they made their way to Danzig, now Gdańsk, in Poland. It was October 1944 by the time they arrived and they were immediately put on barges and sent down the river to Stutthof concentration camp, 21 miles east of the port city. First set up in September 1939, Stutthof was one of the first camps used by the Germans. While prisoners were generally put to work there, more than 85,000 were killed in the camp's gas chamber or by lethal injection. With Hitler's Final Solution in full swing towards the end of the war, the camp commandant even brought in mobile gas chambers to speed up the rate of executions.

Evidence also exists of a small-scale production of soap from the corpses of those killed at Stutthof. One of the leading Nazi doctors, Rudolf Spanner, is said to have taken corpses from the camp to his experimental factory near Danzig. When liberated by the Russians, soldiers found vats full of human heads and torsos pickled in liquid.[16] The subsequent war trials saw seventy-eight of the approximately 2,000 SS guards from Stutthof brought to justice.

Shindy knew that arriving at the camp would mean another selection process where guards would once again isolate those too weak to work. Both her aunties were much taller and would usually get through selections without a problem. But it was different for the slightly built Shindy. As the guards walked along the line, she once again stood on her toes and puffed out her chest in an attempt to look older and stronger. This time it did not work.

'I was picked out and locked in this washroom with all the other children who were the same height as me. I knew what they were going to do with us, we were going to be taken over to the crematorium and we would all be killed. So I jumped up on the sink and climbed out of an open window. Just as I was jumping I saw an SS guard standing there with my two aunts.'

Distraught at the thought of being separated, her two aunts had decided they would rather have gone to their graves with Shindy than continue on without her.

Luckily, and to their surprise, the SS guard allowed Shindy to rejoin them in the camp while the children who were still locked in the washroom were taken away.

The next day the three were on the move again, this time to just outside Hamburg. They were made to walk to a train station and then transported to a camp that doubled as a munitions factory. Shindy was put to work on a lathe making bullets for the Nazi war machine until she poisoned her finger in an accident. As a result she was transferred to a different hut where she made hand grenades, a dangerous and fiddly task that saw one of the other prisoners blown up.

The conditions and treatment at Hamburg were awful, with the same meagre rations and a particularly harsh camp commandant. After twelve hours of slaving away on little food and drink, with the prisoners wanting nothing more than to sleep, the commandant would make them do extra work or drag them outside to stand in the freezing cold.

'We would have to clean our rooms and he used to come round with two SS women looking for dust on the window. I remember once I was up on the top bunk sleeping and he came in and shouted "Everybody out". I was just jumping up when he threw two buckets of dirty water all over me – just because I didn't get up fast enough. I ran and jumped out the window with no shoes on and he made me stand there in the snow all day long.

'He would shout and scream at us like a madman, telling us we were "filthy little Jews" and saying things like "I know where you come from". It got so bad and we were so tired that the foreman of the factory said we were no good to him like this, he said he needed us rested. So they brought in another commandant who was a bit nicer. He told the SS guards that if we had to do twelve-hour shifts then they would have to as well. They were not happy at all because they were used to doing about four hours at a time so they spread a rumour that he was having an affair with one of the girls. They did away with him and got the old commandant back.'

Most of the concentration camps across Europe were run by SS guards, who were known for their poisonous hatred of the Jews and feared for their brutality. In the women's section of the camps it was female SS guards in charge.

'They would compete against each other, they would see who could be the most brutal, it was like they were showing off. If they caught prisoners trying to steal potato peelings – which the guards would throw away anyway – they would give them fifty lashes. The guards would get them in the corridor and bash them as hard as they could. The other guards would have buckets of water ready for when they fainted so they could keep going. They would say things like "Oh you like it, you are not crying" so they would give you fifty more.'

It got so bad in Hamburg that Margit, Shindy's younger aunt, made a knife in an attempt to take her own life. 'She had had enough, you got fed up at times but we told her she couldn't do that. We had to stay together. There were other girls who did commit suicide though, they just couldn't take it any longer.'

Now in the spring of 1945, the Allies were moving ever closer to Berlin. Bomber Command had stepped up its raids on Germany's industrial heartland and Shindy and her fellow prisoners watched from their hut windows as the planes flew overhead. 'The guards would all rush to the shelters but we just watched, we were pleased. We never thought they would hit us.'

By April, many of the senior German officers knew it was just a matter of time before they were defeated. Many went into hiding, in particular the SS who would face severe punishment for their actions during the war. Camps were left in the hands of the more junior guards and in some cases even volunteers. With manpower lacking at Hamburg, most of the prisoners were moved to one of the largest concentration camps in Germany, Bergen-Belsen.

On arrival Shindy was met with the strange sight and sound of a band, dressed in their evening suits, playing cheerfully as if it was some sort of holiday camp. Belsen was anything but. Tens of thousands had been killed there prior to her arrival, with many left unburied to rot in the spring sunshine. If she was in any doubt about the scale of what had been going on, it was all too clear now.

'There were twenty-four of us girls that went into Belsen together. The guards in the lookouts were just randomly shooting people so we stayed close. Inside there were bodies everywhere. In the barracks they were piled right up to the ceilings. On the walk from the railway track to Belsen, the wagons were full of bodies that had been in there for six days; you can imagine what they looked like. My aunt went round turning bodies over thinking she would find her father. It was obviously no use. The SS didn't care at all; on the walk to the camp if someone fell or could no longer go on, they would run them over with their motorbikes.'

But brutality was not the only killer in Belsen. Typhus fever had taken over and prisoners were dying in their hundreds every day. In Hamburg, Shindy had taken some of the cleaning fluid they used at the munitions factory and it was probably only that, which they used to wash their hands with, that saved them from succumbing to the deadly disease.

Belsen, they thought, was to be their new home. But just days after arriving at the camp their old commandant from Hamburg arrived unexpectedly and asked for twenty girls to head back to the factory, as his new intake was not up to the job. Shindy's aunts were called out to return, but she was told to stay at Belsen. But yet again, Shindy managed to sneak in unnoticed and made the journey back. The three could not be separated.

Unbeknown to them the British would liberate Belsen just days later. But even after the camp was in Allied hands, thousands continued to die every day. Many were simply too ill and failed to recover despite medical attention, and others died because they ate too quickly for their shrivelled stomachs.

Shindy and her aunts spent another two weeks back in Hamburg under the close watch of the SS before a deal was signed for their freedom. Swedish diplomat and nobleman Folke Bernadotte negotiated the release of around 31,000 prisoners from concentration camps. He arranged for them to be taken as far north as possible where they were put on ships bound for Sweden. Shindy and her fellow prisoners knew little of the deal, other than they were to board a train. That train was bound for Copenhagen where she remembers being greeted by a German solider.

'He said, "Now you will be free and I will be killed". They opened the wagons at the station and people saw this bread shop. They were so hungry that they ransacked it, the owner had to get out so they could take what they wanted. We were then shown to a ferry that had tables beautifully laid out with cakes and sandwiches, bread and milk. It was gone within seconds.'

It was early May 1945 and the prisoners were taken to Malmo where the Swedish authorities met them on the beach. They were stripped, showered and checked over by doctors before being housed in a sports centre where, for the first time in a year, they had beds and mattresses. They were required to stay there in quarantine in case they had contracted typhoid and it was there, just days after their arrival, that victory was secured in Europe.

'I had been queuing up for food with my aunts in the sports centre when we heard the news. It didn't make much difference, we were free by then.'

Shindy remained in Sweden for a year before getting her visa to come to England in April 1946.

'Our relations didn't understand what we had gone through so the three of us stuck together. To start with, nobody wanted to know about the Holocaust. It never leaves you to be honest, I had a nightmare just two days ago, but I can talk about it.

'Looking back now I cannot understand a world standing by while Germany took over so many countries and went in and killed. Was it because we were just Jews? It is difficult to comprehend how it all happened.'

Shindy eventually settled in Hove and raised a family. Today she keeps few reminders of the war, just the brass ring hammered for her by the Russian prisoner, now barely big enough to fit on her little finger, and her black and white school photograph. The image captures a happy childhood, a time before her town fell victim to Hitler's Final Solution. For Shindy it feels like a lifetime ago, but it is never forgotten.

JOHN BUCKERIDGE

LIFE AND DEATH ON SNAKESHEAD RIDGE

A lot is made of the camaraderie among servicemen who stand side by side on the battlefield. 'A band of brothers' – the famous phrase from the St Crispin's Day speech of Shakespeare's *Henry V*, is often used to describe the unique relationship. But for John Buckeridge, who served as a troop commander with the Royal Sussex Regiment, he felt like more of a father figure to his men. So much so that after being blown up atop an Italian mountain by a grenade, he wanted not to return home or to receive a period of rest and recuperation, but instead he pleaded to be back with his men.

'I felt responsible for them and I wanted to make sure I was with them and that they were OK. We lived in each other's pockets and there was a close bond between us. We had been through a lot together and I couldn't leave, I had to get back to them.'

John, who later went on to become a colonel, fought alongside his men in one of the most brutal and ferocious battles of the entire war. In February and March 1944 he was stationed on a small ridge overlooking a key German strategic point in the mountains of central Italy. Standing between the Allies and Rome was a hilltop abbey called Monte Cassino that dated back to the sixth century. The regiment was tasked with storming the enemy stronghold, but in just two attacks it lost twelve out of fifteen officers and 162 of the 313 men.

Now living with his wife in Cuckfield, the memories of Monte Cassino are ever-present in his mind.

'Even now I think to myself "why me?" How come I survived and so many others did not? I was lucky, I went on to have a good life; I have a lovely wife, two super sons and four super grandchildren. But many did not survive and never got the chance at life that I did.'

John was born and brought up in London, where he got his first taste of the war with the Blitz of 1940 and 1941. The relentless bombing campaign, which resulted in tens of thousands of civilian deaths, 'helped him form his opinions of the Germans'. But despite his eagerness, he was too young to sign up and fight and so instead enlisted with the Local Defence Volunteers (LDV), later renamed the Home Guard. Much like the BBC sitcom *Dad's Army*, most of those who joined were older men, too senior to be sent to the front. For someone to join because they were too young was a rarity and as such the Kensington Platoon found plenty to keep John busy.

'I was a lance corporal and being so young I suppose I was like Pike [Private Pike played by Ian Lavender], although not as stupid. I became an instructor and I learnt all about the Lewis gun and about grenades and mortars. I also experimented with new types of weapons they were trying to introduce because in 1940/41 there were very few weapons in England; we were reliant on the Americans to resupply us. It was a very busy time.'

When not carrying out his voluntary duties for the Home Guard, John tried to live his life as any normal teenager and on his evenings off he would head to Piccadilly with his friends. He knew the bombers would come each night, but he was determined to carry on as usual and enjoy his teenage years.

'We would see the great fires from the Blitz when we went into the city, but life went on. If there was an air raid we would take cover and try and find a shelter, and then as soon as it was over we would get back to what we were doing. I remember one night the bombs were coming down and I ran into the entrance of a shop for cover. The following morning I walked past the same shop I had been in and realised it was a showroom made entirely of glass. Thankfully none of it shattered as I would probably have been killed.

'But we refused to let the Blitz rule our lives, we had to get on as normal and try and enjoy ourselves, because back then you never knew if there would be a tomorrow.'

With John reaching the age for active service, his time for socialising in the West End was about to come to an end. On 12 February 1942, he boarded a train from Victoria station with hundreds of other recruits. Their destination was Chichester where they were to be enrolled in the Royal Sussex Regiment. John didn't have a long family tradition in the forces. His father had been in the Great War, but that was the extent of it.

'If there had not been a war I would not have ended up in the army. I would probably have been a writer or a journalist. I had never even heard of the Royal Sussex Regiment, it was all very alien to me.'

Keen to impress, John had worn his Home Guard uniform, complete with lance corporal stripe and had polished his shoes until he could see his face in them. Along with the other recruits, he was marched down to the regiment's barracks where he came across a steely looking sergeant by the name of Walker.

'He took one look at me and got out his knife. He bellowed, "What are you doing wearing a lance corporal stripe?" and he tore it off my uniform. That was my introduction to the Royal Sussex Regiment and the real army.'

John was made a private, but he was a fast learner and determined to move up through the ranks. He excelled in basic training, which was carried out in and around Chichester before he was posted to the 10th Battalion in Seaton Carew near Hartlepool. Despite not yet having seen action, he was made an instructor and taught new recruits in the ways of soldiering.

But in September 1943, aged just 20, he received his orders for deployment. Such was the fear of spies, he was not told his destination, only that he was to head to Liverpool docks to board a troop transporter. They set sail in a huge convoy with protection from the Royal Navy, with the threat of German U-boats ever present.

'It was a worrying time. Nobody told us where we were going, but we knew there would be U-boats. Before we set off we were told we could not smoke in case anyone saw us and we were not allowed on the deck at night.

'We were basically a slow-moving target and we knew a German torpedo could hit at any point. And it wasn't just from underneath, there was also the threat that dive-bombers would attack from the skies. We were very apprehensive but there was nothing we could do, we just hoped for the best really. We heard the odd explosion, but we made it through.'

They were crammed into the 20,000-tonne troopship *Manna del Pacifico*, which had been fitted out with bunk beds three-high in all the communal rooms. Although unsure of their destination – and if indeed they would make it there given the dangerous waters they were sailing through – there was a welcome distraction for the men. While half the ship was occupied by the soldiers, and a quarter by the entourage of Peter of Yugoslavia (who was in the RAF), the remainder was made up of members of the Women's Royal Naval Service, better known as Wrens. Their quarters were strictly off limits to the army personnel, but boys being boys, those in charge struggled to enforce the rule that led to 'quite a bit of fun' as John remembers.

About a fortnight after sailing out past the Royal Liver Building, the men finally sighted land once more. They had arrived at Port Said, Egypt, at the mouth of the Suez Canal. They did not know it at the time, but they had been part of the first convoy to make it through the Mediterranean – most were forced to sail south round the Cape of Good Hope – for a number of years.

John, who was now a second lieutenant, joined with the Royal Sussex Regiment's 1st Battalion, which had been involved in fierce fighting across North Africa with Lieutenant General Bernard Montgomery.

'These men were experienced and battle hardened, you could see it in them. We were fresh off the boat and all completely green, but we had to mix in straight away because we knew we would soon be in the thick of the action.'

However, there was something of a calm before the storm as the battalion was taken out to Lebanon for ski training, in anticipation of their forthcoming assignment. They had been earmarked to join the Allied forces in making for Rome and driving the Nazis out of Italy. The invasion of the country was key, especially as support for the war among the Italians was waning. A successful landing, it was thought, would remove them from the war entirely. As soon as they held the south of the country, the Germans would also lose their grip on the Mediterranean, which was a key supply route for forces in the Middle East and Far East. Elsewhere, Joseph Stalin was pushing for an invasion of Italy in the hope that a second front in Europe would divert German forces away from the assault on Russia.

The last twenty-one months of John's life had been in preparation for this moment. As a second lieutenant, he was what was known as a troop commander and, at the age of just 20, he was in charge of twenty-five men on the battlefield – a job he relished, but felt enormous responsibility for.

'I got to know all of my men extremely well as we were with each other all day, every day. I was very protective of them as we were a team and I was their leader. But not only did I know them as soldiers, but I got to know them personally, I got to know about their families and where they had come from. As many could not read or write that well, I would be the one who would help them write their letters home and I would have to read the replies when they came.

'I would be there to help them with all manner of day-to-day tasks. For example, I remember the British had these lovely great thick grey socks, which the Americans were very jealous of as they had horrible nylon things. But as a result the men had to darn their socks regularly. Many didn't have the faintest idea how to, so again, it would be up to me to show them. I really was a father figure to those men and there was huge mutual respect. I thought very highly of all of them and it was an absolute tragedy to lose anyone.'

Although he had not undergone extensive training for his leadership role, John had watched and learnt from his superiors in the field. One officer in particular, Ben Dalton, he remembers as being a great influence on his style of leadership. The 'extremely brave and often completely mad' company commander, as he recalls, knew everything there was to know about the art of being a soldier and John watched, listened and absorbed as much as he could.

Help was also at hand from his batman – an army term for an officer's personal assistant. The young soldier named Henry not only acted as his bodyguard, but also his right-hand man, and John was perhaps closer to him than anyone else in his platoon.

Shortly before Christmas 1943, the men of the Royal Sussex Regiment's 1st Battalion were loaded on to landing craft bound for Taranto in southern Italy.

As the vessel bounced across the Ionian Sea and the great naval port came into view, John could not hide his apprehension. But the city had been on the receiving end of an immense bombardment before they arrived and the Germans had long gone.

Over the next few weeks they moved up through the south of the country, along the eastern coastline, until they reached the River Sangro, where the Germans were dug in. It was the first time John and many of the men had come face to face with the enemy and understandably there was great anxiety.

'I soon had a system of sorts to tell how nervous my men were, as the closer we got to the line the more they would use the f word. As we got nearer to the enemy and the explosions got louder and more frequent, every other word would be the f word. I found that was the same with all the other battles I was involved in throughout the war. It was no good me telling the men to stop because it was a release for them and it helped me judge how they were feeling.'

They dug in at what became known as the River Sangro Line and the two sides exchanged fire over a number of days. But the awful weather conditions and strength of both sides' defences meant a stalemate soon developed. After just ten days, John and his men were given orders to make their way west to the site of a Roman Catholic abbey called Monte Cassino.

The small town of Cassino, with the hilltop abbey just over a mile away, was at the far western end of the German's defensive Gustav Line, which ran the width of the country to the south of the capital. If the Allies were to make it through to Rome and take Italy they would have to defeat the Germans at Cassino.

Set on top of a 1,700ft ridge, the abbey was at the head of the Lira and Rapido valleys, with views for miles around. German artillery could pick off Allied targets before they got anywhere near to the abbey and various outbuildings and rocky ledges meant they could dig in, making the strategic point near impossible to take. The Allied generals knew as much and sent thousands of British, American, Indian and Anzac troops to the area in January 1944 to try and make a breakthrough.

'The weather that winter was awful. It was cold and it rained almost constantly, and when it was not raining it was snowing. The terrain was also extremely difficult to fight in. The Germans were alright, they were up out of harm's way, but we had to climb to get to them.

'Even to get up on the ridge was a struggle as they had deliberately flooded the flat farmlands in the valley and the only way to get around was in these big US Army jeeps. A lot of them got stuck and so it was instead a job for the local mules to resupply the men. You would see these poor animals dead in the ditch, sinking with their legs up. It was very unpleasant.'

But the men of the Royal Sussex had no time to worry about the conditions, as on their arrival in the area they were ordered to relieve American troops holding a vital position overlooking the back of the abbey, called Snakeshead Ridge. The position was the highest in the area – even higher than the abbey – but it was small and narrow. From the ridge the men could see into the back of the monastery, but between them and their objective was a heavily defended German position called Point 593, just 70 yards away. They were so close that they could almost hear the Germans talking, and if they dared put their head above the rocky outcrop for long enough, they would be able to see the whites of their opposition's eyes. But if they were to take the abbey, then they would have to take Point 593.

The first obstacle for the men was to make it up to Snakeshead Ridge as they were forced to trudge through the rain for hours, using poorly maintained mule tracks. The Germans knew the area well and had maps showing which paths the Allies would use. And so at regular intervals each day they would line up their mortars and artillery and bombard the pathways. But on the night of 12 February, John and his men made it. And as they watched the weary, ghost-like American soldiers file past them down the mountainside, they wondered what the next few days would have in store.

'I was commanding 13 Platoon, which I kept until the end of the war. We got ourselves in position on the ridge, which was only about 30 yards wide before it dropped straight down. My platoon was at the far end, nearest the Germans, who were at Point 593. They were just a matter of yards away, so it was constant danger.'

The men were at the mercy of the elements, with little shelter to protect them from the freezing winds, rain and snow. All they could do to keep warm was huddle in their sangars, which were small temporary fortified positions made with stones, rubble and whatever else they could find to keep the cold out. There were no tents and in their sangars the men had just a groundsheet and their waterproof gas cape to keep them warm.

'You rarely got much sleep, but the main thing was keeping warm and out of the wet. We just had to get by with what we had. After a week or so of wearing the same kit and not washing, it does get a bit gungy and all you want to do is shower and get some fresh clothes, but to be honest we had bigger things to worry about.'

Up on the ridge, they were prisoners during daylight hours, unable to move for fear of being picked off by German snipers. It was a lesson John learnt the hard way, as one morning while shaving, his batman and close friend Henry let his guard slip for a split second. The crack of a rifle echoed over the ridge and Henry dropped to the floor. He was dead.

'That was a difficult time. I had grown close to Henry, he was a good chap and we got on well. It was not a nice thing to have to experience and I missed him.'

With the casualties starting to mount up, the Allies had to make their move. Debate still surrounds whether the Germans were actually stationed inside the abbey, which would have been a breach of a Vatican agreement that deemed the site strictly neutral and not to be used for any military activities.

There was certainly no denying that the Germans had positions around the holy site, but reconnaissance missions could not ascertain for certain if they were inside the building.

Airmen on one observation flight are said to have spotted Nazi uniforms hanging on a clothesline in the abbey courtyard and machine-gun emplacements close to the walls.[17] As one of the soldiers positioned nearest to the abbey, John is certain that it was used by the Germans. 'Up on Snakeshead we could see right down into the backdoor and I regularly saw them going in and out. I was only about 1,000 yards away from it and I can say with certainty that they were using the abbey.'

The Allies had already launched a number of infantry attacks on the position, but had made little ground and suffered heavy losses, particularly among the American troops. With the enemy so well dug in, the Allied generals knew they had to soften the Germans up and so they reluctantly decided to bomb the historic abbey.

On the morning of 15 February, 142 American B-17 Flying Fortresses, followed by forty-seven B-25 Mitchell and forty Martin B-26 Marauder medium bombers, took off from airfields in the area and made their way to Monte Cassino. John, who had not been informed of the raid, despite being just 1,000 yards from the target, looked to the skies with confusion as he heard the drone of aircraft engines. As the bombers flying in perfect formation got closer, he dived for cover and told his men to do the same. In the next few minutes more than 1,150 tonnes of high explosives and incendiary bombs were dropped on the abbey, reducing it to a smouldering pile of rubble.

'Nobody told us about it, it was a complete surprise. I saw the bomb doors open and then the bombs fall from the plane. If you think about the geography of the area, there is Cassino town, the monastery, Point 593 and then us, all in a straight line. We were directly on the bombing run and the accuracy back then was not what it is now. My men were lucky, but it was a bit uncomfortable I can tell you. It was like being back in the Blitz.'

For a good five minutes a cloud of smoke and dust shrouded the abbey. When it finally lifted, the Allies could see their work. They had succeeded in destroying the building, but rather than exposing the Germans, their intense bombardment had the opposite effect. The enemy's position was now easier to defend than before. If there was doubt about whether the Germans were using the abbey as a shelter prior to the bombing, they certainly were after the raid, with the rubble and blocks of concrete making perfect sniper and machine-gun positions.

There is also no evidence that any German troops sheltering in the building were killed in the bombing run. However, there were casualties, notably up to 230 civilians seeking refuge there.[18] The raid had also left many Allied soldiers injured, with explosions on the granite mountainside sending razor-sharp shards flying through the air. Twenty-four of the 1st Battalion were wounded.

The Allies wanted to take advantage of the raid and the 4th Indian Division was ordered to storm the abbey in the immediate aftermath. But their commanders refused, arguing that it would be suicide to try and take the monastery while the Germans still held Point 593, which looked down on the building.

So that afternoon John and his men, still shaken from their near miss, were called together. They were ordered to wait until darkness and then storm and take Point 593. Given the topography and terrain of the area, it had been impossible for the Allies to carry out reconnaissance and so, despite being so close, they did not know how many Germans held the position. And with the narrowness of the ridge, they could not go over in large numbers. It was down to just one company of three officers and sixty-three men to carry out the raid.

As night fell, they waited anxiously in their sangars, checking their weapons and ammunition. They did not know what they would meet on the other side of the ridge, but they knew many would not return. John briefed his men and made sure everyone understood the plan. They were to use the element of surprise to creep up on the position and take it before pressing on to the abbey.

When the signal was given he led his men over the ridge towards Point 593. Silently they moved forward, weapons raised in anticipation. With each agonising footstep, the granite beneath their feet crunched, but still they had not been spotted. Then, just 10 yards from the enemy's line, the rattle of a German machine gun broke the silence. The Royal Sussex boys dropped to the floor and returned fire, throwing grenades as John urged them to keep moving.

'Because we were on the side of the mountain there was no grass or anything like that, it was granite. And the boots we had at the time were called ammunition boots with metal studs on them. That made quite a noise so it was almost impossible to move forward without being heard.

'We had trained to fire and move then fire and move and so on. It was basic infantry tactics, but it was effective. However, once we had been spotted it was difficult as we were pinned down. Given the landscape and the immense aerial bombardment there were no trees or bushes for cover. It was completely open.

'You are scared, but in the heat of the moment you just get on with it. You know you have a job to do and you just try and stay alive. You also have to persuade your men to do what they have to do as well, it is very easy to get frightened but you can't let this happen – and it didn't.'

John's platoon was engaged in a fierce grenade battle at close quarters with the enemy. The casualties started to mount up, but they had to keep moving and try and take the position.

'There were no personal communications or radios or anything like that. The men had to go with whatever we had said in the briefing before or I would have to shout orders on the battlefield. We only had one radio and that was for me to contact my company commander. But given how cold it was the batteries kept packing in and the only way to get it going was to shove it up my jumper to warm it.'

After a couple of hours of this close-quarters, sometimes hand-to-hand, fighting, John and his men were starting to run out of grenades. Before first light they were told to retreat.

Of the three officers to lead the raid, John was the only one to return. Eighteen of the sixty-three men to go over were also killed, with another fourteen injured.

'We had very nearly taken it, but had run out of grenades, which are crucial for that sort of close-quarters assault. It was a very difficult time for all of us. I was one of the lucky ones really. So many of them didn't come back that night.'

Following the assault came one of John's most distressing jobs as an officer. It was down to him to write a letter informing the next of kin of a soldier's death.

'I felt a lot of responsibility for the men under me and it was always hard when you lost someone. When I had to write to their mother, father or wife I would find it very difficult to know what to say. I had grown very close to these people and I had seen them die. I usually went with words of sympathy rather than anything too soppy. It was one of those things I just had to do.'

Back at Snakeshead, the men regrouped and those seriously injured were taken off the ridge to a field hospital by mule. The men had been badly beaten up, but the generals already had plans for those able to fight on. Another air raid was launched with fifty-nine US fighter-bombers attacking the monastery and surrounding area with an artillery attack also directed at the mountain-top position. But once again the bombardment had not touched Point 593, which the battalion was ordered to assault again that night.

Having analysed their previous attempt, it was decided to take twice the number of men over the top. They would attack on two fronts, with one group approaching from the south while another would attack from the north. Once the point was taken, reinforcements would move forward to fend off an expected German counter-attack – or at least that was the plan.

After running through the drill with his remaining men, John swapped his standard issue officer's pistol for the increased firepower of a sub-machine gun and led them over the ridge once more.

They crept forward trying not to disturb the granite underfoot and again got to within yards of the enemy position before they were spotted. German machine-gunners swept the area as grenades were tossed indiscriminately, spraying shards of rock on explosion. John and his men tried to hide behind what little cover they could find and moved forward where possible.

'They had used Italian labour to build these little caves so they were well dug in and very hard to get at. And they were not just any old soldiers; they were German paratroopers, who were among the best we came up against. They were very good defenders indeed.

'We threw everything at them, but it was hard going. Everyone knew how important that position was. If we could take it, we could take the monastery.'

With the assault at its most ferocious and the casualty count rising, John got pinned down close to the German line. With a number of the British 36M grenades on him, he tried to get out of trouble by launching a volley of the explosives towards the enemy position. In return the German paratroopers threw their stick grenades back at him.

'There is not much you can do in a situation like that. There isn't time to pick them up and throw them back. If you hear one come over, you just have to get down and hope for the best.'

With John lying face down on the ground, he felt a thud on his backside. Realising it was a German grenade he covered his head and waited for the explosion.

'There was a terrific bang and the first thing I remember thinking was how relieved I was to be alive. I felt my legs to see if everything was still there, which thankfully it was. But I was not in good shape, I was bleeding like a pig.'

The shrapnel of the grenade had ripped into John's lower body and he was losing blood at a staggering rate. With the fighting going on around him, he was taken back to the ridge to be assessed by the medic. He judged him to be too badly wounded to be treated on the mountain, so it was arranged for him to be taken down to a nearby field hospital for an operation.

'The only way down was on the mule tracks we had come up on. I was loaded on to this animal and it started on its way, but I kept falling off. In the end I decided I would walk down and I was met at the bottom by one of the army jeeps.'

Despite the ferocity of the fighting, the Germans respected the Red Cross and so, although they had a clear sight of the medical trucks departing for the hospital, they left them alone. Once at the medical facility John was cut out of his bloody clothing before going under the knife. The surgeon removed all the shards and shrapnel he could get to and patched him up before he was sent to recover.

'I was lucky really that it didn't hit anything serious. In recent years I have been to hospital for various things, including having a full body scan. Afterwards the radiologist came to me and said "Mr Buckeridge, something has shown up on our scan, it looks like there is something in there". It turns out there is still a bit of shrapnel in my backside, but it has never given me any problems.'

John had been lucky. The grenade was just a matter of feet away when it detonated and he had lost a lot of blood. But despite having just undergone surgery, all he could think about was getting back to his platoon.

'They were my men and I wanted to be back with them. I needed to be back on that ridge.'

Despite taking more than 250 men on the second assault, the Germans had stood firm once again at Point 593. Of the fifteen officers to lead the attacks over those two nights, twelve were lost. They were followed over the ridge by 313 men, 162 of whom did not return.

After just two weeks, John was back on Snakeshead, but the 1st Battalion was soon relieved and moved to a position known as the Bowl. After a gruelling and costly few weeks on the ridge, they were now thankfully out of sight and range of the German guns.

'We were disappointed that we did not quite make the breakthrough. This battalion had been fighting in Africa since 1940 with the 4th Indian Division and they were very successful. This was the first time they had come up short. But on the other hand, we were relieved to be alive, as many were not as lucky.'

With a death rate of nearly 54 per cent, the battalion was not strong enough to continue to push for Monte Cassino and arrangements were made to take them off the mountain. On 21 March, just days before they would return down the mule tracks, John looked out over the peaks into the night sky. In the distance towards Naples, he could see what appeared to be an extravagant firework display. He was in fact witnessing the last major eruption of Vesuvius, the volcano that 2,000 years previous had wiped out nearby Pompeii. As he gazed to the south-east, lava flowed from the rim and ash clouds shot into the sky.

Just days later on 25 March, John led his men down the mule tracks – relived but disappointed – to the Allied camp in the valley. There they had showers, hot food and were given fresh clothing. For them, the Battle of Monte Cassino was over. It would be another two months and several more costly assaults before the abbey was taken, opening the route to Rome for the Allies.

The breakthrough came after an intense artillery bombardment which was followed by a multi-national joint advance launched by British, American, Australian, French and Moroccan troops among others. However, it was the Polish Army that finally took Point 593 and pushed on to capture the abbey, at the cost of thousands of lives. In the early hours of 18 May, with the Germans in retreat, the Polish flag was raised in the ruins of the building. The men were said to be so battered and exhausted that it took some time to find a few fit enough to climb the last few hundred yards to the summit to plant the flag.

The Battle of Monte Cassino had finally been won after 123 days. More than 55,000 Allied soldiers had been killed or wounded, along with 20,000 Germans. It is regarded as one of the most brutal and bloody battles of the war and resembled something of the stalemate of the First World War trenches.

Meanwhile, with numbers so thin on the ground, reinforcements were sent to bolster the Royal Sussex Regiment, which was to push on through Italy. Just a few months before, John had been in the new recruits' shoes, having arrived in Port Said and been told to join the band of weary, beaten, battle-hardened men. They were green, as he had been, but they would have to learn fast, with the men soon back in the thick of it.

They headed north into the hills, where they spent the spring and the summer fighting smaller battles with the retreating Germans, as they slowly pushed them out of the country.

'There was good morale among the men and we had considerable success moving north through Italy. It was mostly small platoon action and my men fared well. We stayed together and looked after each other. There was a rule that if you were injured three times then you could go back to England, but none of my men put themselves forward for that. The regiment had a good reputation and we did our bit to ensure that continued.'

After crossing the River Rubicon in the north-east of Italy, the Royal Sussex men were told their job in the country was done and they were instead to be sent to Greece.

'Many people don't realise it, but the Germans occupied Greece and we had to move in to kick them out. My brigade was sent up to Thessaloniki in the north where the Greek Communist Party was trying to take over. They were supported by the Bulgarians and of course the Russians were moving across. If they had got into Greece then it would be a very different country today. But we stopped them.'

From November 1944 until after VE Day, John and his men, who had been with him since Monte Cassino, had to be on their guard against the Greek Communist's guerrilla army.

'It has not been widely reported, but I can tell you it took place because I was there. It was a proper little ding-dong war and we came under attack quite often. They would try and take our ammunition and our weapons, but we stopped them. We held firm.'

After the Armistice was signed in Europe, John was taken back to England with a view to being sent out to the Far East. But with the atomic bomb bringing the war to a quick conclusion, he was instead sent back out to Europe, before heading to Palestine.

John and his men had been involved in some of the fiercest fighting of the Italian campaign and in his platoon, which started with twenty-five men, just thirteen remained by the summer of 1945. Monte Cassino had been a baptism of fire for a young man who had never envisaged a life in the forces. However, when the war ended, John was offered the chance to remain in the army and he worked his way up to the rank of colonel. Even after retiring in 1978, he remained involved with the regiment and was an active member and later a president of the Royal Sussex Regimental Association.

Yet of all his thirty-six years in the army, it was those few weeks on Snakeshead Ridge, in the freezing months of February and March 1944, he remembers most clearly. But it is not the conditions, danger and the ferocious bombing raids that are foremost in his mind, but rather his men who he fought side by side with.

JACK LYON

MY PART IN THE GREAT ESCAPE

After months of planning the Great Escape, Jack Lyon queued up in hut 104 of Stalag Luft III and waited his turn to crawl into the hand-dug tunnel, codenamed Harry. Lots had been drawn to decide what order campmates would escape and one by one his friends disappeared beneath the floorboards in the dead of night. All was going to plan until 4.55 a.m., when German gunfire shattered the silence. The 76th man through the tunnel had been spotted by the sentry as he made a run for the woods. The game was up. Jack had drawn lot 79. It had almost certainly saved his life.

We have all seen the film, but few can say that they were part of the Great Escape. Jack Lyon can – and he lived to tell the story.

Born in September 1917, Jack had a good education and got a respectable job, first working for London Gas and then for Shell in their headquarters in the capital. But with Hitler's influence growing in Europe and war looming in autumn 1939, his employers said he was no longer needed and advised him to join the services.

At 11.15 a.m. on 3 September 1939, the deadline for the withdrawal of German troops from Poland expired and Prime Minister Neville Chamberlain declared war. Two days later, aged just 21, Jack signed up to serve in the RAF, not that it had been his first choice.

'I went with a friend to an army recruitment office which was attached to the 4th and 5th Royal West Kents. Where I used to work, a lot of the men were members of the regiment's Territorial Unit, so we wanted to be with them. We got there in good time, but to our disappointment it was closed. Somebody told us the RAF had opened a recruitment office in a nearby pub so we went along and the rest is history.

'People ask me if I was signing up to "do my bit" or to "serve King and Country". But it wasn't really like that. I just wanted to do something different. I had been a pen-pusher for a number of years you see and this was exciting and certainly something different.'

The same day as he enrolled, Jack was sent off to Uxbridge where he collected his uniform and was asked what he would like to do. He was disheartened as the recruitment officer ran through the list of available roles – cook, butcher, administrator.

'Then he said, "Have you considered aircrew? If you pass the training course you will be a sergeant and you will be on twelve and six a day." That was it, there was really no contest so I asked him to sign me up.'

Despite Jack's eagerness, there was no space on the training courses and with the war yet to really begin in earnest, aircrew were not in demand. He was instead sent home with a number of books and told to study in anticipation of ground school.

Christmas passed and it was 29 December when he finally received his orders to report to Downing College, Cambridge, where he remained until spring 1940. But progress through training was slow and there were no vacancies for Jack to be posted to an RAF base. That was until Hitler invaded the Low Countries in May 1940, ending the Phoney War. The Third Reich was now just a matter of miles from the south coast of England and the logjam impeding Jack's progress was soon cleared. Within days he was sent to RAF Kinloss, on the north coast of Scotland, where he trained in air defence.

'I remember I was put on this 20mm cannon, but no sooner had I mastered it, it was taken away and sent down to the South of England with the threat of invasion all too real. It was substituted with a Lewis gun, which had a pan of ammunition on the top. I was given a little bunker, but we were instructed not to fire without the permission of the Ground Defence Officer. Problem was, we neither knew who he was or where he resided.'

Thankfully this was not a problem as, within weeks, Jack was sent south to RAF Burnaston, in Derbyshire, where he would finally start his flying training. He failed the pilot's exam, but trained at the East Midlands base as a navigator before being sent for further practice up in Prestwick, where he was tested in the Scottish Highlands and valleys to hone his navigational skills.

In November 1940 he was sent for a final stint of training at the air armament school at RAF Manby, Lincolnshire, where he came out top on the bombing and gunnery course, earning him a commission as pilot officer. He would end the war as a flight lieutenant.

More than a year and a half after entering the RAF recruitment office with his pal, Jack was finally a fully fledged member of Bomber Command and ready to fly sorties over enemy territory. He was posted to the headquarters of 4 Group, at RAF Linton-on-Ouse, in North Yorkshire, and was made part of 58 Squadron, flying Whitley bombers. He was also assigned a crew and in just his first few weeks at Linton, he got a taste for how devastating and destructive war could be.

'I was in bed one night and I heard the air-raid sirens. I didn't have time to go anywhere so I just stayed where I was. All of a sudden I heard this damn horrific crash. I didn't want to get up because for all I knew I would be going towards the danger. I just stayed put. In the morning I found out the huge explosion was in fact a direct hit on the air-raid shelter, which killed all inside. Eighteen were dead, including some of my original crew and the station commander. For a few days after it was all a bit chaotic and I didn't have a crew at all for a while. It was terribly sad, but that was war. We got on with it.'

Just weeks later, Jack was informed of his first assignment with his new crew. Their target was Boulogne, one of the Channel ports. This short trip was referred to in Bomber Command as a nursery run. Little resistance was expected and it was a typical sortie for a crew embarking on their first mission together.

'I suppose it was a big moment after all that training, but I wasn't worried. This is what it had all been about, I had trained for it and I just sort of took it in my stride. I was very calm.'

Jack and his four crewmembers made it over and dropped their bombs on the occupied French port and returned in their Whitley without incident. Just days later they went on their second nursery run before their first big raid over enemy territory.

Their target was the industrial city of Dusseldorf, in the west of the country, and in particular the marshalling yards near the station. They set off just after dusk and made their final approach towards the target shortly before midnight.

'It was my first major operation and only my third overall, so it was quite something. We had the searchlights scanning for us and when they spotted the plane they would all swing round and you would get, what we called, coned. It would blind the cockpit, which was obviously very bad news for me as the navigator. Once we were coned, it was not long before I started to hear the bonk of shrapnel hitting the side of the fuselage.

'People ask me if I was scared, but there was no time for that. This was my job and I had to find the bloody target. If I was worried about getting shot down

I shouldn't have joined up. All I was thinking was get these bloody searchlights off me, I can't see a damned thing.'

Jack tried to guide the pilot through the heavy fire towards the target, using landmarks on the ground like the Ruhr River and his air speed to judge their exact position. But given the searchlights, conditions and rudimentary bomb-aiming equipment available, it was near impossible to hit the marshalling yards with any accuracy. Once over what he believed was the target, he released the load and the pilot turned for home. It had been a baptism of fire, but they had made it. Or so they thought.

Fifteen minutes into the return flight, the Whitley bomber's port engine caught fire and soon huge flames engulfed it. The pilot deployed the extinguisher, which had little effect, so instead he tried to steady the plane as they approached the Dutch border. Worryingly, in the cockpit, they could not get through to the rear gunner on the radio and so Jack set about crawling through the cramped fuselage to see if he was OK. He scrambled along in near pitch darkness and opened the door behind the wireless operator when he was hit by a wall of flames and smoke.

'It was incredible, I nearly passed out there and then, and I had to quickly grab an oxygen mask and take a few breaths just to recover my senses. We didn't know it up front but the back of the plane was an inferno, we were going down and fast.'

With the reality of the situation now clear, the pilot ordered the crew to abandon the aircraft. As required, Jack went first to make way for the other crewmembers. Calmly he opened the hatch and jumped. But as he exited the plane, disaster struck as he hit his head on the top of the hatch, knocking himself out. The 23 year old, who minutes earlier was returning safely to base, was now out cold, plummeting to his death.

'All I can remember was coming round when my chute opened as it give me a huge jolt. I must have somehow pulled the ripcord. I was incredibly lucky. As I floated down, I saw the aircraft, which was engulfed by flames, circle round before crashing with a tremendous explosion.'

Remarkably all five jumped to safety but were now scattered for miles around. The rear gunner, it turned out, had jumped before Jack, which explained his silence over the radio. The pilot was the last out and he later told Jack that he counted just five seconds from his chute opening to him hitting the ground.

Jack landed alone in a playing field near to the small town of Goch, just a few miles from the Dutch border. The night was silent, but with the burning Whitley lighting up the sky on its way down, he knew it would not be long before they were discovered. He was bleeding heavily and dazed from the knock to the head, when a member of the German version of the Home Guard approached. Jack was worried given that there had been rumours of the mistreatment of aircrew prisoners.

'He appeared out of the darkness riding his bicycle. He didn't say "Fur Sie ist der Krieg vorbei" ("For you the war is over") but had he done so, I would have reluctantly had to agree with him. I couldn't fight my way out of Germany in a flying kit, I wasn't even armed.

'But now the soldier had a dilemma. He had his bike and he had to get me back to the town on his own. He could have held the bike in one hand, the rifle in the other and then got me to walk in front. But in the end he offered me a ride on the crossbar. I thought it would have been churlish to refuse so I got on. It must have been a bizarre sight if anybody had seen us. Had it been caught on camera, I think a print of it would be quite valuable now.'

The kindness of the soldier had taken Jack by surprise, as did the courtesy he was about to receive from a German civilian when the pair reached a row of houses. With Jack still bleeding heavily from the head, the solider knocked on the first house he came across and asked the owner for help. She returned with a bowl of warm water and the solider bathed and cleaned Jack's wound while the woman made him a cup of tea. After finishing and saying his 'dankes', the pair continued on to Goch and Jack was taken to the town's police station where he was met by a Luftwaffe officer the following morning. He had just spent his first night as a prisoner of war. He would spend more than 1,000 more before he would make it home.

First stop for Jack and the rest of his crew, who had been rounded up in the hours since the crash, was Dusseldorf, their target the previous night. They were taken via the train station, which remained intact despite their best efforts, to a holding camp near Frankfurt. He was immediately put into solitary confinement and brought out only to be interrogated by a German officer. All captured airmen were given what was said to be a Red Cross form to fill out. In return their captors said a message would be sent back to their family, informing them of their whereabouts. But in reality it was no Red Cross form, instead a document drawn up by the German intelligence service in an attempt to extract as much information from prisoners as possible.

'For three days they asked me questions, but I didn't tell them anything other than what I was permitted to say: my name, rank and number. We had been told about these bogus forms so I wasn't falling for it. I told the officer as much and he accepted it, there was no effort to force anything out of me. There was a certain respect between the RAF and Luftwaffe personnel, especially at the start of the war.'

Following his time in solitary confinement, Jack was sent to the main compound until an escape attempt by other campmates saw him transferred to another camp called Stalag Luft I, near Barth, on the Baltic coast in June 1941.

His treatment at the hands of his German captors remained decent and, to his surprise, they were put on a civilian train to reach the camp. And while the Western world was in the midst of one of the most destructive wars in history, the class system remained, with senior British officers invited up into second class on the service while those of lesser ranks were down in third. It was a similar story once they arrived at the newly opened Stalag Luft I, with the officers separated from the non-commissioned officers, who were sent to a segregated, more basic, compound. Given his rank, this was the last Jack saw of his crew.

He recalls the camp as being 'quite liveable', describing it as 'Butlins but without the entertainment'. However, the winter of 1941/42 was particularly harsh and Jack's resolve was tested with temperatures plunging to -40°C. But even during the bleakest of winter days, the RAF inmates found ways to create some light relief.

'We flattened out and hosed a large patch of the camp grounds to create a skating rink. We had a consignment of skates sent from the Red Cross in Geneva and we all had a go. I got quite good actually, despite a fall which resulted in a deep cut to my eyebrow. My roommate, Silverstone, managed to break his leg on the rink but the Germans looked after him. He got a steel rod in his leg for his troubles and even got an RAF disability pension.'

For Jack, camp life was monotonous, but bearable. It was simply a case of getting through it and keeping yourself sane and entertained as best you could. Each day would start with a morning roll call at around 8 a.m. with a similar register finishing off the day before the camp huts were locked for the night. With officers not permitted to work under the rules of the Geneva Convention, it was up to the prisoners to keep themselves occupied during the day. But as Jack remembers, there was always something to do.

'We had a library with books from the Red Cross and we had sports and some recreational facilities. There was gymnastics; we had parallel bars and that sort of thing. A lot of men would just choose to jog and exercise around the edge of the parade ground. However, you had to be careful not to go too close to the warning wire in case an over zealous guard misinterpreted your intention. I kept myself busy by reading, I remember one book in particular was by a chap called Clapham, it was called *The Great Railway Age* and was about the birth of the railway in England. It was a great big tome, some thousand pages, so that kept me busy.

I also took Spanish lessons, which came in useful for my job when I took a post in South America following the war.'

Food at the camp was generally basic, but there was enough to go around. The usual fare would be some form of soup with rye bread and the men also got bi-weekly food rations which included bread and pieces of German sausage.

Unlike many prisoner camps controlled by the Axis forces in the Second World War, those run by the Luftwaffe for the RAF were generally well maintained and the guards respected the Geneva Convention.

'There was a real camaraderie between aviators regardless of which side you were on. The guards were fair and decent with us, on the understanding that we would be the same for their pilots captured in England.'

Jack witnessed that mutual respect when, on a fine autumn day, he spotted a German chatting casually with one of the camp's Battle of Britain heroes. But this man was no prison guard; he was a Luftwaffe fighter ace by the name of Franz von Werra. The Playboy-type figure was a national hero having claimed many kills during the Battle of Britain and the Battle of France. However, his extraordinary run came to an end when he was shot down over Kent in September 1940, an event that was the making of his reputation. Not content with sitting out the war in a prisoner camp, he made several attempts at escape, including tunnelling out of a camp in Derbyshire. He then made his way to the nearest aerodrome and pretended to be a Dutch pilot in order to convince the crew stationed there to let him fly one of their Hurricanes.

After being recaptured, he was sent to a camp in Canada, but on the way he leapt from a moving train and travelled south until he crossed the border into what was then a neutral United States of America. He made his way back to Germany via South America and Hitler gave him the Ritterkreuz des Eisernen Kreuzes (Knight's Cross of the Iron Cross). Not only was he said to have improved the lot of British prisoners after telling of his treatment in England, but he also visited camps to chat and reminisce with the pilots he was trying to shoot out of the sky only months before.

Jack would remain at Stalag Luft I until the following April, 1942, when he was selected to be amongst the intake at Hermann Göring's new flagship high-security camp, Stalag Luft III.

Göring, who was head of the Luftwaffe, thought the camp so well equipped and comfortable that prisoners would see no point in attempting escape. And if they did, the design of the facility would mean that they stood next to no chance.

One key feature intended to stop any would-be escapees was the raised huts, which were 24in off the ground, making it easier for guards to detect any tunnelling activity. The camp was near the then German town of Żagań, now part of Poland, and 100 miles south-east of Berlin. It was built on a sandy subsoil and it was thought that the bright yellow earth would be impossible to dispose of if the men were creating a tunnel. The loose sand also made tunnelling dangerous and was expected to put prisoners off taking the risk.

Following previous breakouts at other camps around Germany and further afield in recent months, the Nazis had also chosen Stalag Luft III to trial the use of their new seismograph microphones, which were positioned around the perimeter of the camp to pick up any sound of digging. Escape, it was said, was impossible. Yet in the two years he was there, Jack was involved in two of the most audacious breakouts of the war.

However, his first few months at the camp were miserable, as he suffered badly with a foot infection. News from the outside also suggested that the Germans were heading for victory. It got so bad that he considered an easy way out by 'walking over the wire', a decision which would have seen him shot on sight. Luckily, 'reason triumphed', he recalls. It didn't for a friend of Jack's, Flying Officer Edwards, who one day emerged from his hut and walked slowly and purposely towards the wire. 'Before anyone could stop him, he crossed it and began to climb. The patrolling guard called out "Halt", but Edwards took no notice.'

The guard shot him and his body crumpled, still tangled in the wire. A friend of Edwards', Eric Foster, ran out with little regard for his own safety to free him. But it was no good; he died from his wounds later in hospital.

In autumn 1942, Jack was temporarily transferred from Stalag Luft III to another camp, Oflag XXIB in Poland, where extreme temperatures tested his will once more. So cold were the nights, his boots would be stuck to the floorboards by dawn. There was a successful breakout there, although he was not part of it. Not long after, in early 1943, he was transferred back to Stalag Luft III, where plans were already afoot for an escape.

The breakout, which would become known as the Wooden Horse Escape, was the brainchild of RAF officers Lieutenant Michael Codner and Flight Lieutenant Eric Williams. They had approached Flight Lieutenant Oliver Philpot, who was their hut's coordinator of escape attempts, and the three set about their daring plan.

Prisoners considered it too far a distance to dig from one of their huts to the outer perimeter fence, so the trio plotted to dig a much shorter tunnel right in front of the guards' eyes. They would conceal themselves inside a wooden vaulting horse and while other prisoners, including Jack, vaulted over it, they would dig away underneath, doing a little each day until they had reached beyond the fence.

'The horse was made mostly from the boxes from our Red Cross parcels if I remember correctly. Each day we would carry it out into the parade ground and they had built these little foot rests so they could crouch up inside. It was all very clever. Once on the spot, they would get to work while we vaulted over it. It was a fantastic idea and it worked.'

Only two could fit inside the horse at a time, so the trio took it in turns to do the digging. They lined the claustrophobic shaft with plywood panels and at the end of each day they had to be careful to replace the top of the shaft and topsoil to avoid attention.

For 114 days they carried out this dangerous work, while Jack and his fellow prisoners kept up the game, dutifully vaulting over the wooden horse. Before the tunnel was finished in autumn 1943, Jack was moved to the newer north compound of the camp. It was on 29 October, during a new moon period, that the three decided to make their escape. They all squeezed into the underside of the horse for the final time and were wheeled out to the parade ground, where they began their final scramble through the tunnel. To their relief when they dug upwards at the other end, they were past the fence line and the three scarpered into the woods without being seen.

Assuming fake identities – Philpot as a Norwegian margarine salesman called Jon Jörgensen and Codner and Williams posing as French workers – the three made their way to the nearby station and travelled to Frankfurt. Philpot then caught another train to Küstrin in western Poland and then on to Danzig, now Gdańsk in Poland. There he almost gave himself away after falling and swearing in English. He smuggled himself on to a ship bound for neutral Sweden and upon arrival he was taken to the British Legation in Stockholm, less than five days after the breakout. Meanwhile, the other two made their way to Stettin, now Szczecin in Poland, where they met with members of the Danish Resistance, who took them to Sweden via Copenhagen.

'It was the most successful escape of the whole war there is no doubt about that, all three got home safely which was incredible. I never knew the exact details of the plan, but I didn't need to. In camp, you did not speak about it if you didn't have to, you would certainly never use the word escape. You never knew who was around or who was listening.'

As far as prisoner camps went, Stalag Luft III was a big one. By summer 1944 there were five separate compounds, each consisting of fifteen single-storey huts. In total the camp stretched across 60 acres, eventually housing more than 2,500 RAF officers, around 7,500 US Army Air Force personnel and around 900 officers from other Allied air forces. There was a hospital, football pitches, a Red Cross store and even a theatre.

'Some of the prisoners were very good on the stage, there were some really good-quality productions put on. I remember going to see a production called *George and Margaret*, there were lots of Noel Coward plays and things like that. There were certainly things to keep you occupied, but we wanted to escape.'

From the moment Jack arrived in the north compound, he knew plans were afoot for something big – and so did the Germans. They had what the prisoners called Ferrets, guards trained specially to detect escape attempts. Dressed in distinctive blue overalls, they would enter the compound and search huts without warning, using metal probes to search for any tunnelling activity. There was one Ferret the tunnellers feared more than any other, a corporal known as Rubberneck. He prided himself on scuppering escape attempts and would lurk around the huts listening out for careless talk.

So high were the stakes that newcomers to the camp were treated with suspicion, as prisoners feared the Germans would try and plant spies. Any new arrival would have to be personally vouched for by two existing prisoners who knew them by sight. Anyone else was known as a stool pigeon and they faced extensive interrogation by senior camp leaders and would be followed at all times until they were deemed safe.

For Jack there was no such trouble, with him now something of a veteran of prisoner-of-war camps across Europe. However, there was little talk of the specifics of the escape. It only really became evident that a concrete plan was in place when a fellow prisoner one day took half the slats from his bunk, leaving Jack with less of a bed and more of a hammock.

The escape plan was conceived in spring 1943 by a South African-born RAF squadron leader called Roger Bushell, portrayed in the 1963 film by Richard Attenborough. The former barrister had been shot down in May 1940 in a dog-fight over Calais. He was captured before he had a chance to hide and would spend the next three years in camps across Germany. Escape was regarded as something of a duty of all prisoners of officer rank and Bushell took to his duty with aplomb. Before arriving at Stalag Luft III he had attempted escape twice, the first time cutting through the wire and the second by jumping from a moving train. Most officers realised that even if they made it out of the camp, their chances of reaching England were slim. But it was almost seen as a sport to them, something to keep the mind active and to give the Germans the run-around.

On his arrival at Stalag Luft III, Bushell was already a well-known figure and was made head of the escape committee. His endless enthusiasm and drive were infectious and he gave people the confidence and belief that his wild plans would work. Setting out the blueprints for what has become known as the Great Escape, he gathered the inner circle of the committee together one evening and is recorded to have delivered the following speech. 'Everyone here in this room is living on borrowed time. By rights we should all be dead. The only reason that God allowed us this extra ration of life is so we can make life hell for the Hun … In north compound we are concentrating our efforts on completing and escaping through one master tunnel. No private-enterprise tunnels allowed. Three bloody deep, bloody long tunnels will be dug – Tom, Dick, and Harry. One will succeed.'[19]

Nothing on this scale had ever been attempted before. Other escapes had seen perhaps a dozen men try to get out through tunnels, but the construction of these three would enable more than 200[20], Bushell forecasted. It is thought that more than 600 men were involved in some way in the construction of the tunnels which had their entrances in hut 123 (Tom), hut 122 (Dick) and 104 (Harry). They were dug extra deep, 28ft, to avoid detection by the German seismograph microphones and they would need to stretch more than 330ft to reach the tree line past the perimeter fence.

'Bushell was the mastermind, he was in charge of the whole operation and he was codenamed the Big X. He was very taciturn and reserved, he didn't converse with everybody. He was also a very good thespian and I think that was part of his cover. The Germans knew he was an escaper, but perhaps thought that he was now putting all his efforts into the theatre.

'It was a fantastic feat, so many people were involved in so many ways yet there was not a lot of talk about it, you couldn't afford to because you never knew who was listening. My roommate, a chap called Dennis Cochran, was involved from the start. He was in charge of making contact with one of the German guards to get information relating to train times and identity passes. So as soon as this German chap turned up I quickly found myself somewhere else to go or something else to do.

'Once we had the guard on side, that was it. They only had to help you out with one thing, be it by bribing them or something, and then you had control over them. If their seniors found out they had been helping you then they would face the firing squad, so we had the power over them.'

Jack wanted to be more involved. So when a fellow prisoner approached him one day with an offer, he gave the nod. He was to become vital for the surveillance work, or stooging as it was called.

'I would work day and night watching out for German guards while the others were working away doing whatever they were doing for the escape attempt. I would usually peek out through a crack in the hut or through one of the shutters that wasn't fastened properly. It was hard, intense work, in that you could not let your attention falter even for a second. If you messed up then it could compromise the whole operation.'

Across the north compound hundreds of others were doing similar jobs. One of the most important roles was that of the diggers. These fearless and immensely flexible men had to dig away in a space no bigger than a coffin, with makeshift tools and little oxygen. They were at constant risk of the tunnel collapsing and it was only a sophisticated air pump system that kept them alive. Incredibly nobody was killed in the construction of the tunnels, but many were injured.

Then there were the penguins, who discreetly deposited the bright yellow soil from the tunnel on to the parade ground using an ingenious method. The prisoners would fill thin, long bags with the soil before slipping them inside their trousers. When they took to the parade ground, they would pull a cord that released the soil slowly out of the bottom of their trousers, allowing them to spread the earth without raising suspicion. Such was the weight of the full bags, the men would totter along like penguins, hence the nickname. Jack was considered for the job, but given his height (5ft 5.5in), the bags would have dragged along the ground.

Also key to the operation were the forgers who created fake documents, passports and identity cards. They relied on those who bribed the guards for equipment like cameras, ink and official papers. There were also map makers who tried to plot the local terrain and tailors who created authentic-looking farmers' dress and civilian clothing to help the men blend in once they reached the other side of the fence. The sheer scale of the operation was staggering and the fact that they managed to keep it from the guards was testament to their sophisticated surveillance system.

What could not be bribed from the German guards, the prisoners had to find from around the camp. The inquiry following the escape resulted in the following list of missing items: 4,000 bed boards, 1,370 beading battens, 1,699 blankets, 161 pillow cases, 635 palliasses, thirty-four chairs, fifty-two twenty-man tables, ninety double-tier bunks, 1,219 knives, 478 spoons, thirty shovels, 1,000ft of electrical wire, 600ft of rope, 192 bed covers, 3,424 towels, 1,212 bed bolsters, ten single tables, seventy-six benches, 246 water cans, 582 forks and sixty-nine lamps.[21]

Each man was given a cover story. Some were to be traders and travelling sales-men, others Polish farmers. Jack, given his schoolboy French, was to be a French worker – of which there were many in Germany at the time.

'I was given an identity card which didn't have a photograph, but it probably would have passed a cursory inspection. My French wasn't great but I was told to do my best and pretend I was from Brittany or perhaps a French Canadian. The Germans wouldn't be able to tell a good French accent, I was told. I was also handed a couple of maps, some German currency, about £20 worth, and I had a uniform, a sort of workers' smock that was made for me.

'When people think about the Great Escape they should not think about the film, it was incredibly inaccurate. For a start there were no Americans involved, they were all moved to a different compound months before the breakout. In the film it is also glorious sunny weather, which was certainly not the case. It had been an awful winter and although it was March, there was still snow on the ground. At night the temperatures dropped to -5°C to -10°C. I knew my chances were virtually nil but I thought I would give it a go.'

Jack continued his surveillance work for months, with progress in the tunnels kept strictly on a need-to-know basis. By the time of the escape, just one of the three – Harry – was still open. Tom had been discovered by a German Ferret and destroyed months earlier, while Dick's surface exit point became the area used for a camp expansion.

In the build up to the escape, those waiting to take part entered a ballot to decide who would be given the chance to make their break for freedom. The men were split into two groups. Firstly those who spoke good German and who were experienced escapers with the best chance of making it home. Those who had made the greatest contribution to the tunnel were also included in this first group. These men got the best forged papers and documents, were near the front of the queue and would travel by train out of the area.

The second group was made up of what were called the 'hard-arsers' who only had rudimentary papers and who planned to make it on foot by night while resting in the day.[22] They made up the rest of the 220 who were set to break out. Jack, a hard-arser, was issued with number 79.

On 24 March 1944, with Harry now 336ft long and stretching – it was thought – to the tree line beyond the perimeter fence, the signal was given. It was around midday and Jack was walking the parade ground when a fellow prisoner approached him and simply said 'Tonight, hut 104'.

His first task was to shave off his beard, which would give him away on the outside. In order not to arouse suspicion he had only a small window of opportunity for the trim, between dusk and the huts being locked shortly after – by which time he would need to be in hut 104.

'It was a quick job and my face was rather sore after, I can tell you. I remember it was a cold night and there was still snow on the ground, but I made my way calmly over to 104. Inside, I was allocated a place and told not to move and to keep quiet until I was called, it was all very organised.'

At 10.30 p.m. the first man scrambled down the 30ft shaft and started to make his way along. With their maps in hand and going over their cover stories, the prisoners slowly shuffled forward as each man went down into the tunnel. There was an eerie, nervous silence until the camp's air-raid siren sounded. The compound lights went out, including the lighting they had installed along the tunnel with stolen cable. The raid slowed down the escape, but still the men filtered through. On the other side of the tunnel the front diggers were struggling to get through the final section of frozen ground. When they finally emerged, to their horror they found they were just short of the tree line. But with the forged documents relating to the current date, they could not put the escape back in order to dig the last stretch.

Now, with a distance of open ground to cover before reaching the safety of the trees, each prisoner would have to wait at the top of the tunnel for the patrolling German guard to pass. This also slowed down the carefully timed schedule, with just a dozen making it through each hour, compared to the expected one every minute. Those at the back of the queue were told that they were unlikely to make it before daybreak, but Jack was informed to get ready.

'I didn't speak to anyone, I just sat there. I wasn't nervous though, why should I be? A lot of work had gone into it, but it was now or never, there was no point getting anxious about it.'

He shuffled closer and closer to the front of the line as the hours passed. At 4.55 a.m., lot number 75 had made it out the tunnel and into the trees – Jack had number 79. New Zealand Flight Lieutenant Michael Shand was next and he waited at the mouth of the tunnel for the sentry to pass. In the woods, Wellington bomber pilot Flight Lieutenant Roy Langlois was watching the guard and waiting to give Shand the signal to go. To his horror, the guard deviated from his usual path, passing right by the mouth of the tunnel. Langlois tugged the signal rope, in an attempt to tell Shand to stay put. But the message was misunderstood and Shand made a run for it, only to emerge at the feet of the startled guard. He shouted out and raised his rifle before firing at the scampering Shand. Luckily the bullet whizzed past his head and he and Langlois disappeared into the darkness. The guard blew his whistle and dozens of soldiers leapt from their beds, grabbing their rifles. The searchlights were beamed down on the tunnel exit and the dogs were released.

Meanwhile two other men were at the end of the tunnel and in the panic made a run for it. Squadron Leader Robert Frederick McBride was apprehended at rifle point as soon as he emerged while New Zealander Len Trent, who had received the Victoria Cross, made a dash for the trees before throwing himself to the ground under heavy gunfire. He slowly got to his feet and surrendered before the pair were taken back to camp at gun point.

Back in hut 104, they had heard the gunshots and knew the game was up. Men who were already in the tunnel scrambled back and threw anything incriminating into the stove. Jack was desperately close to getting out and had it not been for the mix up at the other end, this may have been a different story.

Following the war, Jack conducted research of his own into the escape, only to discover that he may have been the victim of some queue jumping back in hut 104.

Group Captain Len Trent, who had been the last man out the tunnel, was behind Jack in the ballot, but went through as number 79 – Jack's number.

'I couldn't believe it; he must have hijacked my number and jumped the queue. To be honest it was probably a good thing, given what was about to happen. While Trent was caught at the trees I could have made it with the others. It is not worth thinking about what could have happened then.'

It was half an hour before the Germans traced the tunnel back to hut 104. A guard was put on the door to stop anyone getting out and the men were called to the parade ground in the morning. Of the 220 men expected to escape, 76 had made it through the tunnel and into the trees.

'We were stripped to our underwear on the parade ground and searched; it was bloody cold I can tell you. The Germans seemed at a bit of a loss to be honest; they couldn't believe what had happened. There was a sense of disappointment that we hadn't all got out, but it was a boost for morale, particularly for those who had been behind the wire for a long time.'

Jack was given twenty-eight days in the 'Cooler', made famous by Steve McQueen and his baseball in the Hollywood film. However, given the huge queue of men handed solitary confinement, he never had to serve his time. As punishment the theatre was closed down, otherwise life in camp continued as normal. But just days after the escape, terrible news started to filter back about what had happened to their former campmates.

With Stalag Luft III dubbed beyond escape, the breakout was a huge embarrassment to the Nazis. Vast resources were diverted to the region to round up the escapees and Hitler, incensed by the insult, ordered those found be executed. This was unprecedented and against the terms of the Geneva Convention, which stated that solitary confinement was the maximum punishment for an attempted escape. Göring and other senior officers tried to calm Hitler down, arguing that such retaliation might result in similar reprisals for German prisoners. The Führer eventually decided that fifty escapees should be shot.[23]

The order was given and sent through to the Gestapo, who rounded up the escapees. Either alone or in small groups they were then driven – under the pretence that they were heading back to Stalag Luft III – to remote locations where they were ushered out of the vehicle and told to stretch their legs. Then, with their backs turned, the Gestapo officers shot them at point-blank range. Among the fifty was the Big X, Roger Bushell, who was shot near the German city of Saarbrücken. Jack's former roommate, Dennis Cochran, who gleaned information on trains and bus timetables from the German guards, was also killed on 31 March, just days after the breakout.

Just three made it home, Norwegian pilots Per Bergsland and Jens Müller, and Dutch pilot Bram van der Stok. The Scandinavians made for Stettin, where they were smuggled aboard a boat bound for neutral Sweden while Bram van der Stok escaped to Spain with the help of the French Resistance.

'We were all just stunned; we never thought they would be shot, that had never happened before. The mood in the camp was pretty low after that. The German guards as well felt shame, they had nothing to do with it, this was the work of the Gestapo and the SS. Shortly after we had an auction to raise money for the dependents of those who had been murdered, and the Germans went along with it as well. I bought a little wooden box, which had belonged to a man called Tom Kirby Green. I think I bought it for £25 or something like that.'

Life went on at camp, but the murders had taken the wind out of the prisoners' sails. Summer and autumn came and went with no further escape attempts. But with the Russians gaining ground fast, the Germans were forced to move the prisoners west and in early January they embarked on a mass forced march.

'We were going for perhaps five or six days, we had no idea where. We eventually reached a place called Sprenberg where we split. My group was loaded on to cattle trucks and we trundled westward for another four of five days until we arrived at a town not far from Bremen. From there we were taken to a camp called Marlag und Milag Nord, which had housed Royal Navy and Merchant Navy officers. It was very poorly equipped, a dreadful place.'

For six weeks Jack remained there until, with the Allies crossing the Rhine and getting ever closer to Berlin, they moved once more. They headed north-east until the end of April, by which time they could hear the heavy artillery as the Allies crossed the Elba. Not wanting to be taken prisoner by the Russians, the German Army in the west of the country signed an armistice at the start of May, just days before the complete surrender on the 8th.

After 1,069 days in captivity, Jack was a free man and on 9 May he was flown out of Germany, landing in Dunsfold in Surrey.

Seven years earlier he had joined the RAF by chance. He had been a navigator in Bomber Command and involved in two of the most famous prison escapes of the war.

'I had joined up as I wanted to do something different and exciting and my war years were certainly that. During that time everything stood still, the seasons came and went but that was it. Suddenly I was six years older and was to go back to my job at Shell.

'In the camp I had learnt to make do and mend as they call it, that stood me in good stead. Camp life also taught me to be satisfied with what you have and I think that is important for everyone to learn. But my story isn't one of heroics, these things just happened.'

PATRICK DELAFORCE

FROM GOLD BEACH TO THE GALLOWS

On a glorious midsummer day in 1943, promising cricketer Patrick Delaforce had just taken his seventh wicket for only seven runs. They were record figures for the captain of the army team, who was leading his side against Wrotham village in Kent. He should have been ecstatic, but something wasn't quite right.

'I felt awful. Here we were playing in this sweet little village and I had just got my best ever bowling figures. But I knew it was not their best side, all their players were probably over in Europe getting killed. I knew I had to get out there.'

Only 19 at the time, Patrick was nearing the end of his training and within months he would be on a landing craft bound for Normandy. He could scarcely have imagined what he would experience over there. From the horrors of the battlefield as the Allies pushed into Germany, to the utter devastation and depravity of the concentration camps, Patrick witnessed humanity at its absolute worst. Now in his nineties and living in Brighton, he remembers it as if it were yesterday.

Born into a wealthy and proud family, his lineage can be traced back to the 1300s. Originally from France, the Delaforces made their money in the wine industry and on moving to England they worked as spies, notably for King Henry VIII. Later generations owned hotels in Dover and Calais – the only crossing point to the Continent before planes and the Channel Tunnel. From these vantage points, they kept tabs on the comings and goings of any suspicious characters and reported back to London.

Patrick's dad, Victor, had fought in the First World War and was awarded the Military Cross for his bravery in battle. However, Patrick was never supposed to enter the forces; as the only son he was destined to take over the family's wine business, Delaforce Port, which continues to this day.

In preparation for a life in business, he was sent to top boarding school Sandroyd in Wiltshire, where his classmates included two Spanish and three Yugoslav princes, one of whom was to become Peter II, the last king of Yugoslavia. From Sandroyd he was sent to Winchester College, where he would remain until he was 18 in 1942.

'I had a good time there, but it was hard. It prepared me for what I would encounter during the war. I was beaten many times by the prefects, which wasn't nice but it helped to toughen me up. I got a good education and I made good friends. I have fond memories looking back on it.'

With the outbreak of war in September 1939, the family port business took a back seat as the Delaforces answered their country's call. His father was a colonel based at Supreme Headquarters in Brussels while his uncle, John, was in the secret Special Operations Executive (SOE) working out of Portugal and in the Portuguese colonies of Mozambique and Angola.

Patrick, then aged 15, was still at Winchester College where he was being prepared for life as an officer in the army.

'All the big public schools took their war training very seriously. You had a choice of army, navy or air force, but you were generally expected to join up. At Winchester we had what was called the OTC (Officers' Training Corp) and while there I learnt how to strip a Bren gun, how to fire a rifle accurately and how to deal with a 2in mortar. I knew what infantry battle drill was and we had manoeuvres up on the Hampshire Downs.

'We were all young soldiers, we never questioned it. It was an exciting time, none of us really expected to survive the war, but you just got on with it.'

After finishing school in 1942, the 18 year old was sent for six weeks' basic training as a squaddie in Crosby, north of Liverpool. Training continued at Queen's University in Belfast, before a short posting to Catterick Barracks in Yorkshire where he was assigned to the Honourable Artillery Company.

By now it was 1944 and the plans for the Allied invasion of Europe were advancing rapidly. Patrick was sent down with the other new recruits to a holding base near Seaford where they awaited their deployment.

'There was a huge backlog of troops in the South of England: Americans, British, Canadians. We knew the invasion was coming, but we didn't know when or where. It was terribly exciting and something quite special to be part of. I wouldn't have missed it for all the tea in China.'

On D-Day plus four (10 June 1944), he left Seaford in a landing craft for Arromanches to help with the push through Normandy.

'I remember arriving at the harbour, which was not quite finished, and I had to leap like a frightened gazelle from the landing craft. I had to negotiate a gap of about 5ft to get into the water and then ashore and I can always remember the officer who was there, said, "Careful, we don't want you mincemeat just yet". That was the kind of dark humour that got us through.'

With the Allies making good ground in Normandy, Patrick was told to report to the small French city of Bayeux, some 6 miles inland. While awaiting his orders, he spent three weeks doing specialist training for what he was to face over the coming months, in particular dealing with booby traps and mines.

'There was something of a jam in Normandy at that time with so many thousands of soldiers over there. We were pushing on as fast as possible, but there was only so far they could go before coming up against resistance. It was frustrating because I just wanted to get going, but there was nothing I could do about it.'

Patrick had been trained for three jobs as an officer in the Honourable Artillery Company. On the battlefield he would act either as a troop leader, a gun position officer or a forward observation officer, known as an FOO.

He was a troop leader for much of the early months after landing in Normandy. The 'dashing role', as he describes it, would see him in charge of thirty-two men, sometimes even more. He would command them from his tank, halftrack or other armoured vehicle and lead them cross-country in support of infantry units. His navigational skills were key to the role as he would not only have to know where he was on the map to within an inch, he would also need to be ready to fire on a target with pinpoint precision within seconds of the order being given. As a troop leader he also had responsibility for setting up defensive positions when the armour was not moving, which could include positioning machine guns and making sure there were no blind spots from which the enemy could attack. Each troop was made up of four self-propelled artillery guns, two halftracks, two Bren gun carriers, two tanks and four or five support vehicles – all of which he would have overall responsibility for.

The second role, that of gun position officer, was the one that he performed the least. The 'lynch pin' of the operation, as he describes it, they were in charge of the four vitally important self-propelled guns in the troop, know as Sextons. These 25 pounders provided the main long-distance firepower with a range of up to 7 miles. As such they were often away from the sharp end of the action and the role was the safest of the three.

'It was a vital position, but not one if you wanted medals or if you wanted death and glory. For that you could spend a few days as a forward observation officer.'

The most dangerous job of the three, the forward observation officer or FOO would be required to travel at the head of the armoured troops – sometimes at the head of the whole British Army – to see what lay ahead. It would be the FOO's role, with the help of a radioman assigned to him, to relay information about German forces and other obstacles. He would also be required to give quick and accurate coordinates for the rest of the artillery to fire on if needed.

'I had some pretty hairy moments as an FOO and was badly injured twice. We had a few sick jokes in the army to keep us going and one of them was, if you were doing your job as an FOO properly, then you would end up killed. Well, I almost did. So I must have been doing alright.'

In Normandy Patrick was part of the 11th Armoured Division, which was made up of Sherman tanks and, towards the end of the war, Comet tanks, as well as armoured halftracks and the Sextons.

His troop would usually go into battle alongside an infantry regiment and launch coordinated attacks on the German lines, fortified towns and bridge crossings.

'It was all very tactical and good fun really. I'd had a lot of training so I knew what I had to do. You always had to out-think your opposition. The general rule was, if your enemy could see you, then you would be killed. I had been trained up to the eyeballs by that point and I was ready to put it into practice.'

He would not have to wait long and three weeks after arriving in Bayeux he received the news he had hoped for. Along with the 11th Armoured Division, he was to embark on his first assignment, Operation Bluecoat. Their objective was to capture vital strategic ground in Normandy and in particular Mont Pinçon. At 1,188ft (362m) it was a high point in the region that the Germans were doggedly defending as the Allies pushed on.

'They fought like tigers the Germans; they were fantastic defenders. But we really gave it to them. We were fighting day and night but we eventually made it through. It was a real triumph and my first taste of action, I loved it.

'I was only 20 and I was acting as troop leader and my men were hanging on my every word. But I had been trained for it, I knew what I was doing and I was confident. A lot of the men under me were older, but age never really came into it during the war.'

Bluecoat was a key victory for the Allies and Patrick and the 11th Armoured Division pushed on for a good week following its conclusion, driving the Germans east. Above them, the RAF ruled the skies, with the remaining Luftwaffe occupied by the Russians to the east. However, as Patrick soon found out, it was not just the enemy he had to be worried about.

'You had these gung-ho young RAF chaps who were flying their fighters with not much opposition at 400mph, which is one hell of a lick. They would see units on the ground and just open fire and sometimes we were on the receiving end of it. Each of our vehicles had a large star on the roof to show that we were the liberators. I don't know how they could have missed it. They would just come back and say "Sorry chaps, didn't see you there". We asked our superiors what we should do about it and they said if anyone shoots you, you bloody shoot them back. That certainly gave them a fright.'

They continued to push the Germans east out of France and into Belgium. Now September 1944, Patrick's next major flashpoint would come as the Allies attempted to liberate Antwerp. They came under heavy fire from the occupying force, but it took just a couple of days for them to make the breakthrough and free the historic city. The reception they received from the people of Antwerp was like nothing Patrick had ever experienced. Girls threw themselves at the soldiers, they were invited into homes for tea and brandy and crowds lined the streets. Patrick was later given the Belgian Medal and was made an honorary citizen.

Key to them taking the great city was the assistance they received from members of the Belgian Resistance, who, like their French counterparts, fought bravely for many years while under occupation. But their resistance did not go without punishment, as Patrick found out first-hand.

'As we were moving into Antwerp with the Germans beaten I was waved over by members of the Resistance. They said they had to show me something, but I didn't have time. I told them I would get left behind, but they pleaded with me and said they needed someone to witness what had happened. That was my first real taste of what the Germans had done.'

Patrick was taken to Breendonk, a fortress about 5 miles south of the city. The grey stone stronghold had been turned into an SS prison and concentration camp.

'I remember it very clearly even today. The place had been turned into an abattoir for humans. The SS and the Gestapo between them had butchered – literally butchered – dozens upon dozens of Belgium Resistance fighters, particularly because they knew the British were coming. The SS left a trail of blood all the way through northern France and Belgium, but they didn't care.

'The thing I remember quite clearly was the smell of blood. You would not think blood smells of anything, but when there is so much of it there is a distinct smell. You don't really get them any more, but if you went into a really old-fashioned butchers it was like that, only fifteen times worse. It was a disgusting smell, it really was. I can picture it now, there were great big black pools of it, it was just awful, but I couldn't do anything. I just had to say to them "Right, I have seen it. I will tell my superiors."

'They tortured those poor men for information and the SS just killed for kicks. The Germans had done their slaughter and buggered off.'

Only after Antwerp had been liberated were the true horrors of Breendonk exposed. It is estimated that fewer than 10 per cent of the 4,000 prisoners to have been kept there over the course of the war, survived. Within the walls there was a gallows, execution pole and an almost medieval-style torture chamber, with metal hooks and other barbaric contraptions. The inmates were fed barely enough to keep them alive while they were expected to carry out back-breaking work seven days a week. Given the extreme hardship, those who were sent on to larger concentration camps such as Auschwitz were ordered to the gas chamber on arrival due to their condition.

In charge at Breendonk was the camp commandant, SS officer Philipp Schmitt. Even for the standards of the SS, he was considered particularly brutal. On arrival at the prison, new inmates were forced to stand outside in the courtyard and face the wall. They were told to remain motionless, often for hours, with any movement severely punished. He was known to make regular use of the camp's torture chamber and would set his German shepherd dog, called Lump, loose to savage the prisoners.[24]

One survivor of Breendonk told how a Jewish boy was so sick that he was unable to continue working. As a punishment they threw the boy, who could not swim, in the moat that surrounded the fort. He struggled for more than fifteen minutes before drowning.[25]

'They really were beyond the pale, the SS. They slaughtered those poor fellows in there and just left their bodies piled up. When I was called over to look inside I had no idea what I was going to witness. That stayed with me, it made me angry.'

But there was no time for Patrick to dwell on what he had seen at Breendonk, with the 11th Armoured continuing to push the Germans out of Belgium and into Holland.

Back in England, more than 40,000 paratroopers were preparing to be dropped into the north of Holland, for what became known as Operation Market Garden. The goal was to secure a number of key bridges to enable the British Army to gain access to Germany over the Lower Rhine. It was thought if they could get into Germany's industrial heartland, it would bring about the end of the war.

On 17 September the signal was given and gliders and planes set off in their dozens from airfields across England. The drops were made over two days and Patrick and the 11th Armoured moved in to act as protection on the right flank.

'When people think of Market Garden, they think of the poor wretched Airborne Division getting clobbered, but in fact the whole of the British Army was involved in a huge triangular offensive. We had five or six days of fierce fighting during which we were in danger of being surrounded. We were firing on a 180-degree range, which is not ideal at all. There was a fear that we could be cut off.'

The Germans had armour in abundance in the area. And while for most people their Tiger tank was the biggest concern, it was a piece of artillery with a rather less fearsome name that worried Patrick more than anything.

'They had this mortar which had eight revolving barrels and a little siren on it which let off this terrifying sound when it was fired. We called it the Moaning Minnie and it did a hell of a lot of damage. When you heard it you knew you were in trouble. I remember one time when we were with the Monmouthshire Regiment (infantry) and they were being bombarded by these Moaning Minnies. They were calling for us to return fire, but it was nearly impossible to hit them with any accuracy because they were so easy to move around that the Germans fired and then immediately changed position.'

The Allies captured several bridges between Eindhoven and Nijmegen, but ground forces were delayed by the demolition of a bridge over the Wilhelmina Canal. Over in Arnhem, the British 1st Airborne Division had come up against a far greater force than they had anticipated and had only managed to hold one end of the bridge.

Reinforcements did not arrive in time and they were forced to retreat on 25 September. The defeat ended hopes of bringing the war to an end by Christmas.

In just a few short months Patrick had been at the sharp end of some of the fiercest fighting of the entire war. But not once did he shy away from the action or show any sign of nerves.

'It is very difficult to describe, but I put it down to that famous corny phrase, a stiff upper lip. I'm afraid that did apply. Officers never wanted to show anything other than total confidence and we were born and bred to do that. If you were a squaddie you had to have confidence in your superiors, you didn't want them to be saying, "Oh my God, what are we going to do next?" After all we were there to lead them, push them, chivvy them and persuade them. I think that came from my genes to start with, but also from my schooling, it taught me that one could absorb a lot of punishment.'

Patrick and the 11th Armoured continued to push on, fighting numerous smaller river and canal battles in Holland. That was until a deadly blast put the buffers on his war. Having served as a troop leader throughout Normandy and Belgium, he was assigned as an FOO in Holland, which saw him positioned in front of the rest of the armour in order to plot targets for the artillery.

'It was the autumn and I was travelling in a Bren gun carrier in the midst of these woods. A Bren gun carrier is a bit like a baby tank but without a top to it so there isn't as much protection. They were used quite often by FOOs. With me I had a sweet chap called John Smith. Such a lovely, simple name and he was such a nice man from Liverpool. He was very popular in the battery and a very good footballer as well. He was driving and I was in the passenger seat standing up with my field glasses trying to see what was happening ahead. Then all of a sudden: bang. We hit a double teller mine (German anti-tank mine) and I was thrown out of the vehicle. Poor John Smith was blown to pieces, he didn't stand a chance. He was sitting there one minute driving me and the next he was gone.

'I don't know how long I was knocked out for but when I came round the Bren gun carrier was burning furiously. I was a real mess. I had broken ribs, a broken arm and a dead leg. The mine was right underneath poor John. If it had been a few inches the other side it would have been different. I was mildly unpopular after that because he was such a well-liked man and he had been blown to pieces while I had survived.

'I have always said to my daughters, don't expect life to be fair because it isn't. It wasn't for John Smith that day and it never will be.'

With Patrick severely injured, he was taken away from the frontline to Brussels and an officers' hospital to recover. He met up with his father who was based at the headquarters in the city and was nursed back to health. But just weeks later, in November 1944, he was back at the front where he rejoined his men in Holland. And despite his brush with death, there was no slowly easing him back in.

'No mollycoddling and no pampering. I was sent straight back out as an FOO, despite getting blown up the first time. It was the best thing for them to do, I needed to get back on the horse and that's what I did.'

Patrick was posted to the Inns of Court Regiment, who were holding a large farm near one of the key rivers in Holland. Again travelling in a Bren gun carrier, he would help seek out and identify enemy targets for the artillery to fire on.

'I remember that first night after I had gone and introduced myself to them, all hell broke loose. The Germans launched a huge mortar attack and it was raining down on those poor chaps. They had no real protection on this farm, so they just had to hold tight while I radioed back for help.

'I remember I got through to the battery and requested ten rounds a gun on 100 yards away from where we were – that's where I believed the Germans were firing from. Then to my horror a fruity voice came on the phone and said "Well young Delaforce, what do you think you are up to?" It was my colonel, Robert Daniell, he was something of a bon viveur and always had a slightly boozy voice, this time more so than usual. I don't know why he was answering, I had never spoken to him before and he would never normally speak to a young pipsqueak like me. I think he was probably having a boozy supper with his cronies. I said to him, "We are being bombed, mortared, the casualties are mounting up and the farm is on fire. But other than that we are just fine." Then I asked for my own troop to target the enemy position. "Oh," he said, and you could almost smell the brandy, "we can do better than that" and he ordered the whole regiment to fire on the position.

'I ran back to the Inns of Court boys and told them to belt up because we were in for a rough ride. Then the shells belted down, it was a tremendous attack. At daybreak we all went out armed to the teeth, but the Germans had gone. We had killed a dozen or more and they had probably lost a dozen more wounded. We had hit them hard and it had hurt them.'

Despite the intense bombardment, they knew the Germans would be back as the farm was on a key strategic high point. In order to help them defend against counter-attacks, Patrick's superiors sent him a Sherman tank. They were also joined by a group of Canadian paratroopers left over from Market Garden who offered their assistance.

'They were big hairy brutes and they were just longing for a fight. They decided they would that night go over the river and attack the two villages the Germans held. They went off in their boats and then came back at about 1 a.m. They were celebrating, it had all gone well and they plied me, on the eve of my twenty-first birthday, with Armagnac or whatever they were drinking at the time. It was all great fun.'

But the following morning, on Patrick's twenty-first birthday, the fun stopped. The Germans were furious at the audacity of the Canadians to attack their position at night. So they hit back with everything they had. With mortar and artillery shells raining down on them, they all hurried for cover and waited it out.

Patrick jumped in the Sherman tank and closed the lid before doing what most 21-year-olds do on their birthday: he had a birthday drink.

'I remember turning to the others in the tank and saying to them, "I don't like this one little bit, so do you know what we are going to do?" they all looked rather worried. "You are all going to drink to my health." I had a flask of whiskey with me, which I still have to this day, and we shared it between us with the shells falling all around us. The noise was terrific. It was a birthday I will never forget.'

Patrick and his men fought a number of smaller river battles along Holland's waterways in the winter of 1944. For his bravery in liberating the millions of people in Holland, he received the prestigious Bronze Cross of Orange Nassau, which he was given after the war at a special ceremony at the Royal Palace in The Hague.

The Allies continued to press on into 1945 with Patrick and his men at the sharp end of affairs. A series of huge offences were launched, with first Operation Veritable and then Operation Blockbuster forcing the Germans back past the Maginot Line and to the Rhine, which was their last real line of defence.

Veritable, which took place between 8 February and 11 March, was a long and bloody struggle with bad weather and terrible conditions underfoot making it difficult for the 11th Armoured Division to move forward. Operation Blockbuster was their final push to the Rhine. With the weather and terrain more favourable for the armour, Patrick was in the heart of the action once more.

As the Germans retreated, the Allies kept the pressure on, soon forcing them back to the crucial River Aller. It was during the battle for this key waterway that Patrick received the first of two mentions in dispatches.

Again working as an FOO, in early April he was sent out with his tank crew ahead of the British Army at a key crossing in the river. The rest of the army was held up at a bridgehead, which would not be repaired until the next day. He was tasked with crossing the river and setting up in a small wooded area to help warn of any German counter-attacks.

'I said, "Fine, no problem" and the officer told me, "Don't worry Delaforce, we will soon follow behind you". Over the other side there was a road going through a thick wood. It went straight on for about half a mile and then it abruptly went at a right angle along the river. We gingerly went over and set up near the road and the infantry installed their anti-tank guns. We got out and set about having breakfast and I radioed back to say all was well and I let them know on the map exactly where we were.

'Then all of a sudden the peace and quiet was shattered by these two loud clangs. We jumped up to see what was going on and right there in front of us was a dirty great big Tiger tank.'

The Tiger was among the most feared of all the war machines the Nazis produced. At almost 70 tonnes and with 7in-thick armour at the front, it was near impossible to destroy. It had taken out the two anti-tank guns supposed to be protecting Patrick and now it was bearing down on him.

'The sound of the thing was tremendous, I had never been up close to a Tiger before, but the engine was deafening. The rest of the army was too far behind to help and I had to do something because I couldn't let it destroy the bridgehead, which was vital to the army crossing and continuing the advance.'

With the Tiger rumbling towards him at speed, out of the corner of his eye Patrick spotted a motorbike dispatch rider heading his way.

'It was a tough brute of a man called Gillies, he was a lance bombardier and he had come over to see what on earth was going on. The Tiger had just destroyed the two anti-tank guns with ease, killing and wounding the men operating them. There was no use taking the tank on so we set off on foot and ran to the trees. We had to distract it and save the bridgehead. I had my Sten gun and my pistol and Gillies thankfully had a Projector Infantry Anti Tank (PIAT) launcher, which could do some damage to the Tiger.

'We ran in the woods and we tried to give the impression that there were many more of us and Gillies tried to get a shot. He only really had one go at it and because the trees were thick, he couldn't get a clear sight.

The Tiger followed them, trying to pick the pair out through the branches. His heart pounding, Patrick kept running, but could hear the terrifying sound of the turret – and gun – turning to point towards him. They both knew they stood no chance and would almost certainly be killed. But crucially they had distracted the tank crew and moved the Tiger away from the bridgehead.

'It was well capable of killing us and if it had had infantry soldiers on the back we would have certainly been killed. But thankfully, and to our immense surprise, it all of a sudden turned back and headed up the road. You could almost feel their anger, they must have been thinking "Those bloody stupid Brits, what are they playing at?" We were incredibly lucky.'

Patrick ran back to where his breakfast remained untouched and called in a battery target on where he thought the rest of the Germans would be. The next day, when they had enough infantry over the bridge to make a meaningful advance, they went to see what the damage was. Twenty had been killed and the rest had fled.

'That was a particularly hairy moment, anything could have happened. It is pathetic and pompous to say, but I couldn't do nothing. I had to act. But I was lucky. I was lucky Gillies turned up with a PIAT which they would have seen and feared and we were lucky that they hadn't got supporting infantry, which they should have had.'

Aller was taken and they moved on to the River Weser, which the Allies proceeded to cross. Since landing in Normandy almost a year earlier, Patrick had witnessed horrors on a daily basis, but nothing could have prepared him for what he discovered in April 1945. With the 11th Armoured Division forcing the Germans to retreat, they were approached by a group of Nazi officers who negotiated a truce and an exclusion zone around a camp they claimed was in the midst of a typhus pandemic. The camp leaders said they would hand over the facility without a fight, provided the guards were given twenty-four hours to escape. The British agreed and they continued forward, unsure as to what they would find.

'I remember approaching and we were sprayed all over with this white DDT anti-typhus powder. It was put down our socks, trousers, in our hair and down our backs.'

The convoy continued up the road and the men arrived at the gates of Bergen-Belsen concentration camp. Inside the 12ft barbed-wire fences were some 60,000 political prisoners, many Jewish. More than 13,000 corpses remained unburied and those who lived were half starved and half delirious.

'I remember arriving outside the gates in a Sherman tank. I just remember seeing all these rags scattered all over the place. But when I looked closer I could see that they weren't rags, they were bodies – thousands of them. The stench was awful – it will never leave me. It was a rotting smell. It was rotting flesh. They were hardly alive; there was little expression on their faces. They were walking dead, it was just awful.'

Accounts from members of the 11th Armoured Division are among some of the most harrowing of any during the war. Captain C.K.O. Spence recalled how, upon seeing the British liberators, some inmates ran towards the fence in despera-tion. Some of the soldiers pushed through what chocolate or cigarettes they had, which caused a mad scramble.

'The ragged band fell upon them with ferocious energy,' he recalled, 'and when everything had been seized some were left dead or dying on the ground, torn to pieces by their comrades for the sake of chocolate or cigarettes. The stench is still in my nostrils.'[26]

One of the first journalists inside the camp was broadcaster Richard Dimbleby, father of BBC stalwarts David and Jonathan. Describing the day as the 'the most horrible of my life', his vivied description of what he witnessed shocked the world.

'Here, over an acre of ground, lay dead and dying people. You could not see which was which. The living lay with their heads against the corpses and around them moved the awful, ghostly procession of emaciated, aimless people, with nothing to do and with no hope of life, unable to move out of your way, unable to look at the terrible sights around them.

'A mother, driven mad, screamed at a British sentry to give her milk for her child, and thrust the tiny mite into his arms, then ran off, crying terribly. He opened the bundle and found the baby had been dead for days.'[27]

While most of the guards had fled for their lives, some had remained – many of them defiant. Patrick came across some still clenching their guns and even pointing them at the dying prisoners, while others performed Nazi salutes upon seeing the British soldiers. But with the truce in place, there was nothing he could do. Yet, for some it was all too much to take.

Lieutenant Colonel Robert Daniell was one of the first into the camp after ramming his tank through the front gates. What he witnessed inside, he said, changed him for the rest of his life. When some of the remaining guards tried to stop him, he shot them dead with his pistol. He continued further into the camp and came across a 150-yard trench filled with naked bodies. With his pistol still drawn, he heard gunshots in the distance. He followed the sound until he came across six members of the Hitler Youth torturing would-be escapees. They were shooting the men in the groin and women from behind. He raised his pistol and shot four of them with his remaining ammunition.[28]

Patrick surveyed the scene, one that would stay with him for life, and waited for the British medics to arrive. It was then that he came across the three ringleaders of the camp, who had committed some of the most appalling war crimes in history.

'I remember seeing them at the front gates. They were the three main villains and they were just standing there, watching us. There was Josef Kramer, the camp leader; Irma Grese, an SS warden; and the camp's doctor, Fritz Klein. We couldn't do anything because we had made a solemn British promise, we had to let them get away.'

Kramer, or the Butcher of Belsen as he was dubbed, was in the SS prior to the war.

He was first a guard at the Natzweiler-Struthof concentration camp in modern-day France where he gassed eighty Jews, and sent their skeletons to be housed in the Anatomy Institute at the Reich University of Strasbourg. In 1942 he was promoted and later transferred to Auschwitz, where he was put in charge of the gas chambers. There he was responsible for the deaths of thousands.

Even by the standards of many of his peers, Kramer was known to be a harsh taskmaster, with little or no compassion for his prisoners. Even his own men were said to try to avoid the orders he would give them, such was their brutal nature. He arrived at Belsen and was made commandant in late 1944. Not long after, he gained his nickname, the Butcher.

One survivor, Olga Lengyel, described a 'strange gleam' in his small eyes and said he reigned over the camp like a 'madman'. She told of one occasion when he threw himself at an unfortunate woman for no particular reason and with a single stroke of his truncheon shattered her skull.[29] When there was an uncontrollable epidemic of diarrhoea amongst the camp's prisoners, his answer was to starve them.

Irma Grese, meanwhile, was known to the prisoners as the Hyena. The former dairy worker had become obsessed with Nazism and joined up after finishing school. She rose through the ranks quickly and soon found herself at Auschwitz, where she selected the prisoners for the gas chambers. She was moved to Belsen in 1945.

Survivors told how Grese wore jackboots, carried a pistol and a plaited whip, and was always accompanied by a vicious dog.[30] They said that she derived sexual pleasure from beating the female prisoners with her riding crop, some of whom she beat to within an inch of their lives.[31]

Such was her notoriety, it is claimed she had a lampshade in her room made from the skin of three female prisoners – although this has never been proven.[32] She was meticulously groomed, with custom-fitted clothes and she wore copious amounts of perfume as she walked around the camp, beating and mocking the dying inmates. When the British arrived she was just 21 years old.

The camp doctor, Klien, had also worked at Auschwitz before being sent to Neuengamme concentration camp near Hamburg and then Belsen. Klein made no secret of his motivations. When he was asked how he justified his actions with his obligations as a doctor, he said: 'My Hippocratic oath tells me to cut a gangrenous appendix out of the human body. The Jews are the gangrenous appendix of mankind. That's why I cut them out.'[33]

The three camp leaders, along with forty-four other guards, were arrested by the British and tried in a court of law. With no German lawyer willing to defend them, fearing their reputation would be ruined, it was up to British Army officers to carry out the task. The guards argued they were simply following orders and were not aware of the full extent of the horrors.

Kramer, Grese and Klein were all sentenced to death and hanged by British hangman Albert Pierrepoint on 13 December 1945.

'Nobody knew anything of these concentration camps; we had absolutely no idea before that day. I think more were killed at Auschwitz, but in a way I think Belsen was worse. Auschwitz was a murder camp where you were gassed and killed; you were put out of your misery. In Belsen you died through neglect and mistreatment. It was a slow, painful death for them. Belsen was a blot in human history. I will never forget that day; those things stay with you and they shape you as a person. From that day on we had a new anger about us, we got more and more careless let's say as we went on.'

Unlike Auschwitz, which was largely preserved so future generations could understand its history, Belsen was burnt to the ground in a bid to forget the horrors. But there was no time for 21-year-old Patrick to ponder over what he had witnessed, as there was a battle raging up ahead and a war to win. Within hours they rolled out of Belsen, leaving the army doctors to do what they could.

The Allies pushed on and reached the River Elbe. The end of the war was in sight and everybody knew it, but the Germans continued to defend their position, sometimes until the last man. In the battle for the key river crossing, Patrick worked on foot as an FOO. In what were to be the final days of the war, they would prove to be some of his most dangerous.

'We were working our way across these huge farmsteads, far larger than any of the farms we have back here. They had these big buildings, barns, stables and cellars, which the Germans would hide inside. I was there with just my Sten gun and it was pretty close combat stuff. They were sometimes just 15 to 20 yards away; it certainly got quite hairy.

'They were retreating and they knew it was just a matter of time before the war was over, but nevertheless they kept firing and taking pot-shots at our poor boys. That really infuriated me. They had no reason to go on, they should have just surrendered and spared more bloodshed.'

It was when advancing through one of these huge farms on the edge of the Elbe that Patrick gained his second mention in dispatches. With his artillery behind him, he moved up to support the King's Shropshire Light Infantry.

'We found this big house right on the edge of the river and I got up to the first floor to see if I could call in some targets for our boys. I opened the window and I was astride it looking out over the water. I could see them all streaming across the bridge so I called in an attack.'

Unbeknown to him, as he had been radioing the battery, a German soldier with a grenade launcher had tracked him through his sight. A huge explosion rattled Patrick's eardrums and threw him backwards. The grenade had landed just feet away and shattered into countless fragments. Seven ended up inside him, two of which remain to this day.

'It was a hell of a shot, there was blood everywhere and it had hit my arm badly, as well as the side of my head. I called for help and our medic, a man called Cree, rushed over. He prized as many of the pieces out as possible, which was extremely painful, but seemed to give him some pleasure. A couple of them he couldn't get to, one of which is still in the side of my head. He was a sweet chap, Cree. I remember him joking as he took them out. "Now Patrick you look pretty washed out," he said, "but this should make a good iron tonic."

'The battle went on up ahead, but I was pretty badly shaken up. That was really the end of my war. I was sent off to Brussels to recover and while there, Victory in Europe was declared. I'd had a good war, it was a real adventure, but I was lucky. A lot of very good men died and I lost a lot of good friends from school.

'But I don't think it is like most people imagine. When people ask me about the war they say, "Patrick, how did you feel about it all?" They want to hear the emotion, but there was no emotion, that wasn't in our psyche. You had to be confident and strong and fairly intelligent and know your job, there was no time for anything else. If somebody got wounded or killed that was tough, but you got on with it.'

Following the war, Patrick's beloved 11th Armoured Division was disbanded and he was transferred to the 7th Armoured Division, Montgomery's Desert Rats, where he served as an intelligence officer. While the world was at peace for the first time in six years, Patrick was about to start perhaps the most important job of his military career. He received a call to say his services would be required in Hamburg for the war trials of guards from the nearby Neuengamme concentration camp.

'We had been set up in this grand old theatre in the city, which was one of the last buildings left standing after the bombing by the RAF. There was a judge advocate, who was there to make sure we abided by international law, and then myself and two other officers.

'There was a colonel, a major and then myself, aged just 21. All of us were under 30, but that was what it was like by the end of the war. We had no real legal experience, but we had a lot of common sense. We were up on the stage of this theatre and they would bring the concentration camp guards in one by one, flanked by soldiers, for us to try. They were all complete rascals, but we had to try them fairly.'

Established in 1938, Neuengamme was run by the Nazis up until it was liberated in 1945. During those seven years, some 106,000 prisoners passed through the gates, of which more than half died. Unlike Auschwitz it was not an extermination camp, although it is said many were gassed there. Instead, extermination came through hard labour, brutal conditions and lack of food, shelter and medical provisions. Prisoners were put to work making bricks in the main camp, while others were sent out to satellite camps in the area. It is estimated that more than 50,000 died as a result of the conditions and hardships, and like most others of its kind, it was run by the SS.

The camp mainly housed Jews of many different nationalities, but also communists, homosexuals, prostitutes, Gypsies, Jehovah's Witnesses and Resistance fighters. As well as beatings and shootings, it was said that in 1942, more than 200 Russian prisoners were gassed there with prussic acid.[34]

'We were in that theatre for a whole week, getting through as many of them as we could a day, usually twelve or thirteen. They would come up one by one and say their piece. There were two interpreters to make sure we got an accurate account of what they wanted to say and then they would have their legal representative speak on their behalf. None of the German lawyers would represent them, so it was down to the poor British officers, which was not a nice job for them to have to do.'

While some continued to pledge allegiance to Hitler and the orders that they had been given, most attempted to distance themselves from the horrors for which they were being tried.

'They would try all sorts of things; often it would be "It's not our fault, we were obeying orders". That was a tricky one, but we would just say, "Too bloody bad, they were bad orders, you were in the SS and you were butchering these people, so down you go." They were all guilty, they were all there and they were all part of it, it was to what extent.'

The main evidence Patrick was presented with was what was called the Totenbuch, translated as Book of the Dead. Each camp kept this record of who had died, when and supposedly of what. Along with the military records of the men standing before them, the two pieces of evidence gave Patrick and his fellow judges a record of the numbers of those who died, when they died and at what level of seniority the officers were at the time.

'The stupid buggers should have destroyed the thing. They ran off and left it and that was the evidence we needed. The book didn't say things like "shot in the back of the head" or "beaten to death". Instead it had things like records of twenty, thirty, forty-odd people dying in a single day because of "heart failure". It was ridiculous, they were almost taking the mickey.'

When deciding on their fate, which was a decision between death and a certain number of years in prison, Patrick had to speak first. As the most junior in age and rank of the judges, it was thought that his judgement could be swayed by his superiors if he went after them.

'That didn't bother me at all. I was there and I had a job to do. I had absolutely no problem with sending those sods to their deaths, not after what I had seen at Breendonk and Belsen. Once we knew they were SS, they were doomed. They had ultimate responsibility for the camps, full stop. They butchered those poor people; they did it for kicks. If one of the camp doctors came up before us, he would not stand much chance either. There was evidence of them not only killing prisoners, but also carrying out experiments on them, injecting them with all sorts and even trying out mustard gas and other things. They were appalling.'

The following year, having been promoted to captain, Patrick was selected to take part in another war trial, this time in Oldenburg in northern Germany, where he sent another seven concentration camp guards to their deaths.

'That was an important time for me, I felt that justice was finally being done.'

But justice had not been completed and weeks later Patrick was required to witness the final phase. Dozens of war criminals had been sentenced to death and were being held in cells across Germany ahead of their executions. British hangman Albert Pierrepoint was flown in especially for the task, which was to be carried out in the small town of Hamelin, made famous by the children's story the *Pied Piper of Hamelin*.

Pierrepoint had entered the family trade, with both his father and uncle having also been hangmen. The source of many books, TV documentaries and even a film, he was known for his professionalism, efficiency and strange quirks.

'I never really got to speak to him, but I certainly watched him work. He was very thorough and very professional. He liked to do thirteen a day for some reason, in the time between breakfast and a late lunch. He was doing his job and I quite wanted to go up and give him a pat on the back.

'We were put in this cinema, a very ugly utilitarian cinema which had been renovated by the British Army and cleared up. It had a big stage and the gallows had been specially erected in the centre. They would stand on the stage with a noose around their neck and then there was a trapdoor and they would disappear in a flash and that would be it. I had to sign a document to say I had witnessed what had happened.

'I had been selected to see those from Neuengamme, who I had sentenced to be killed. My only regret was that I didn't get to see the Belsen lot. I had been just yards away from Kramer, Grese and Klein when we liberated the camp and I saw their nasty work first hand.'

The prisoners were brought in one by one, in their uniforms, ready to meet their fate. There was no ceremony, no chance for last words or any hysterics. It was quick, clinical and professional.

'I think that most had been sedated somewhat because there was no kicking and screaming. They went up to the stage and then bang, they were gone and the next one came out. One or two of them came out and said "Heil Hitler" and we would say "Heil Hitler to you too, you can say that wherever you are going now". But that was it, there were no hysterics.'

Patrick watched thirteen war criminals, most of them members of the SS, put to death that day. 'This was retribution, after what I had seen. I had no problem with it at all, in fact I was glad. These people were rats, and what do you do with rats, you kill them. Justice had been done.'

Patrick had come a long way since walking from the field at Wrotham Village Cricket Club in 1943, wishing he could be part of the action. Still only 21, he had helped liberate millions in Europe from the clutches of Nazi Germany. He had killed and watched his friends be killed and had been among the first to witness one of the most appalling crimes in human history. His experiences would have broken many, but he returned to his beloved England and stoically helped rebuild the country in which we live today.

MAURICE MACEY

SPITFIRES, SKYLARKS AND THE CATERPILLAR CLUB

On 14 August 1944, Warrant Officer Maurice Macey was flying his sixty-fourth sortie over enemy territory. He had just unleashed his Spitfire's machine guns on a line of Germans tanks outside the French city of Argentan when an explosion shook the fuselage under his feet. His right knee jolted upwards, hitting him in the chin and seconds later his cockpit was an inferno.

With the flames rising all around him, his training kicked in and he released the canopy before bailing out. His legs were badly burnt and as he floated towards the earth, he heard the sound of rifle fire as a troop of Germans in the field below started shooting. But despite facing what appeared to be the 21-year-old's untimely end, he did not feel fear, sorrow or pain. Instead he felt calm and at ease as the soothing morning song of a skylark filled his head.

'I have no idea where it came from,' Maurice, who later moved to Westham, near Eastbourne, said. 'But in that moment it was all I could hear, the beautiful sound of that skylark. I wasn't thinking about anything else. I was relaxed.'

Maurice was born in Eastbourne in 1923 and his family lived in nearby Langley, which at the time was little more than a dozen houses. Farmland surrounded the hamlet and those born locally would usually go on to tend the nearby fields. However, from an early age, Maurice had different aspirations. When he was just 11 years old he watched in amazement as a strange bird-like machine appeared in the skies above his house. As it got closer, he realised that it was in fact an early monoplane, which thundered overhead before coming in for a forced landing just a stone's throw from his front door. Fascinated by what he had witnessed, he rushed over to see the strange flying machine up close. It was Maurice's first encounter with an aircraft – it would not be his last.

In the years that followed, Maurice would often be found craning his neck skywards to see the weird and wonderful machines up in the clouds. So, aged 14, when a member of the local flying club at Wilmington asked if he would like to join him in a Tiger Moth, there was only ever going to be one reply. He spent little over an hour in the skies above East Sussex, but that was all he needed. From that moment on he was hooked.

'There was just something about it. This was something new and exciting and daring. But I just felt so calm and relaxed up there and never felt worried at all. From that point on I just wanted to fly.'

At the outbreak of war, aged just 16, he joined the Air Training Corp (ATC) where he would learn all of the basics, from Morse code and ground navigation, to the theory of flight. He was a fast learner and was soon awarded his ATC Proficiency Certificate, which was seen as the first step to being accepted into the RAF.

For his RAF training he was posted out to Rhodesia, now Zimbabwe, where he could hone his skills away from the dangerous skies of northern Europe. And for his initial few weeks in Africa he was back in the aircraft he had first flown at Wilmington, the Tiger Moth. Before long he had moved on to the faster and more advanced Harvard and would go up with instructors and practice aerobatics, air-to-air combat and night flying. Due to the urgent need for fighter pilots, Maurice was taking a three-year course in just one year. But he took it in his stride and in early 1944 he was awarded his wings.

'It was a proud day. That had been what I had wanted from an early age and I had been working incredibly hard. It was intense completing the course in such a short amount of time, but it was what I wanted to be doing. I couldn't wait to get back and do the job for real.'

But Maurice would not be heading home just yet, as after two weeks' leave, during which he visited Victoria Falls in nearby Zambia, he was posted to Egypt and introduced to the Spitfire. It was the aircraft all the young men wanted to fly. It was the fastest, most agile and had the greatest firepower. Youngsters had pictures of the aircraft on their walls and, following the Battle of Britain, it had become something of a national treasure.

'It was what I had always dreamt of; there was nothing else like it. I can remember the first time I got in the cockpit very clearly. Those days there was no dual control so you did the classroom lessons and then you go up on your own. It was quite daunting, but from the moment I was up I felt relaxed. It fitted me like a glove and I felt at one with it: man and machine. Once I opened that throttle and heard the roar of the Merlin engine as I hurtled down the runway – there really is nothing else that compares.'

Following training on the Spitfires, Maurice was posted to Fighter Command headquarters in Cairo, before being sent to Cyprus with 127 Squadron. It was there that, after many months of training, he would head out on his first operational flight.

'It was memorable to say the least – but perhaps for the wrong reasons. We were sent out on what was called an offensive sweep. We flew over the Mediterranean looking out for any enemy aircraft. It was a regular thing and it would often result in dogfights, so I had to be on my guard. There was obviously some distance to cover so we carried enough fuel for about 500 miles. The Spitfire had a fuel capacity of 90 gallons and we worked on a basis of around a gallon a minute. We often also carried an extra drop tank of fuel underneath the aircraft, which would allow us to fly for around three hours in total.

'We had been going for quite a while and had not seen a single German so I radioed to suggest we head back. I asked how far we had to go and the reply was thirty minutes. However, my fuel gauge was showing I had just fifteen minutes of flying left. There was a certain amount of panic, especially as it was my first operation, but I just tried to conserve as much fuel as possible. I called in the Air Sea Rescue Service in case I had to ditch, as it was going to be a close-run thing. But after about twenty-five minutes, thankfully the runway came into sight. I brought it down slowly and instead of doing the usual circuit before landing I came straight down. Halfway down the runway my engines cut out. It had been very close and this could have been a very different story.'

Despite his near disaster, Maurice's superiors had noticed his talent and had no hesitation in sending him back up at the next opportunity. He continued to carry out the morning patrols across the east of the Mediterranean into March 1944. But with most of the Middle East and North Africa now in Allied hands, it was decided his skills were better served in northern Europe.

He was posted to RAF Lympne in Kent where 127 Squadron was given the latest Spitfire, the Mark IX. In Cyprus he had been flying Mark Vs, but the new model had been brought in to compete with the Luftwaffe's Focke-Wulf FW 190. Fitted with either the Merlin 61 or 63 engine, the Mark IX had more horsepower (1,690) than its predecessor, could go higher (43,000ft) and faster (408mph). It was also better armed with 20mm cannons and 0.5in machine guns providing the firepower. He would soon need all the firepower he could get, as before long he would be in the thick of the action.

'The main thing was that I had confidence in the aircraft. It was a lovely bit of equipment, really first class to fly. For me it was superior to the 190, so that gave me huge confidence when I was up there. It never let me down and I think that is testament to the design.'

From flying relatively quiet morning patrols over the Mediterranean, Maurice was now being scrambled once, twice, sometimes three times a day to intercept enemy fighters, escort Allied bombers or go on bombing raids himself. The action was non-stop and for the 21 year old, it was something he had to adapt to quickly.

'We lost pilots, of course we did. You went up and you didn't know if you were going to come back, but you had a job to do and you got on with it. We tried not to get too close to each other, as you never knew what would happen in a few hours time. However, there was great camaraderie and of course you couldn't help but build close relationships with those around you when dealing with high-pressure situations together. In particular I was very close to a chap called Peter Clarke and we were together throughout the war. We remained the best of pals for seventy years and we would often reminisce about those days. Sadly he died in January 2015, but I will always remember him and our times together.'

These bonds were formed in the crew room and mess of airfields across the south-east of England, as the men did what they could to cope with the daily business of life and death together. For many of them the worst part was waiting to be scrambled. Maurice could never truly relax, but he did his best by reading or keeping his mind occupied by playing bridge. But when the call came in, everything would stop. The men would run to their aircraft where the ground crew would be waiting to get them up in the air as quickly as possible.

'Everything would happen so fast that you never really thought that much about it, you didn't think about being scared. If we were lucky we would be told where to go and what we had to do before we went off, otherwise it would just be a quick message over the RT (radio telephone). We would usually be told to head off to a certain part of the French coast, where we could expect to encounter a squadron of 190s or whatever.'

One of the RAF's great advantages in the Second World War was their development and use of radar. Thanks to comprehensive coverage, which stretched across much of the English Channel, the fighter squadrons based in the south-east were usually given early warning of approaching enemy aircraft.

'Once in the general area it was a case of trying to find them. I was known by my colleagues as Hawk Eye, as I had very good eyesight and would normally spot them before anyone else. Then it was all about positioning. You couldn't let them get on your tail; you had to get behind them so that you could get a good shot. But you didn't have much ammunition either, you had to be sparing with it.'

Spitfire pilots only had around fifteen seconds worth of ammunition and so the pilots could not afford to be trigger-happy. The key was getting behind your opposite number so that they could not shoot you. This is where the Spitfire's great agility came into its own, as it could outmanoeuvre most others. Once behind the enemy it would take just a short, sharp burst of the guns to bring them down. But surviving in the air was about more than just aircraft specifications and skill – it was also about holding your nerve and mental strength.

'I did have a few close calls and it was scary at times, but we were well trained and I think often that took over. You couldn't think about what might happen too much, you had to focus on what you were doing. Otherwise you would not make it back.'

Maurice had become experienced in the art of air-to-air combat, but in 1944, RAF fighter pilots were also up against a new enemy, the V1 rocket or the Doodlebug as it became known. In essence it was an early version of a cruise missile and it wreaked havoc across the south-east of England and in particular London. Hitler had his best scientists working on the creation throughout the war and in 1944 the pilotless petrol-fuelled flying bomb was unleashed. The Führer predicted that it would turn the tide of the war in his favour, as while before he had risked men to bomb cities, now he could cause the same damage, but without the loss of life.

They were launched from ramps stationed along the French coast and with a wingspan of 16ft they had a range of up to 250 miles. At 2 tonnes, of which 2,000lbs was explosives, they struck fear into the British public unlike anything else in the enemy's armoury.

The British knew Hitler had been developing a new advanced weapon, but it was unclear what to expect. Members of the Royal Observer Corps (ROC), who were stationed along the south coast primarily on the lookout for enemy aircraft, were told to be on guard for anything of note. It was in the early hours of 13 June 1944 that an attentive ROC sentry spotted a bright yellow glow in the sky heading towards the Kent coast. He called his seniors to tell them what he had seen. Minutes later the rocket ran out of fuel and plummeted towards the village of Swanscombe, 20 miles to the east of central London. Over the next few months more than 10,500 V1s were sent over to the south coast of England, resulting in 22,000 casualties.

They worked by being set on a course, usually headed for London, with enough fuel to reach the capital. Those on the ground would hear the terrifying drone of the V1's pulse engine overheard. However, it was when the drone cut out they had to worry, as the rocket was about to start its descent to earth. But the RAF had a plan to tackle the menace of the V1. By calculating their average altitude and their speed, Spitfire pilots were able to get in position as they approached their target. Then, before the V1s ran out of fuel, the pilots would carefully fly alongside and tip the rocket with their wing, causing it to go off course and most likely end up in the Channel.

'It was a difficult and very dangerous job. It was quite a skill when travelling so fast to fly up alongside it and gently tip the thing with the end of your wing. They were sending these things over to bomb Eastbourne, so I had to make sure we stopped them. I couldn't let them destroy my home town.'

Other sorties would see Maurice escort bombers over to occupied France and Germany to provide protection against Luftwaffe fighters. The Spitfires also carried out smaller raids themselves, as instead of the overload fuel tank, which had saved Maurice's life when he was in Cyprus, a 500lb bomb could be attached to the underside of the fuselage.

Although the load was far less than that of a regular medium to long-range bomber, the Spitfires could go in low and fast and hit with greater accuracy. As such, their targets were not great cities but instead troop trains, convoys, bridges, enemy ships and in particular, the V1 launch sites.

'The spring of 1944 was a busy time and we would go on these short bombing runs, two, sometimes three, times a day. We would be told the target, go over, drop our bomb and then get back as soon as we could. I remember on one such occasion we escorted about half a dozen American bombers over to France so they could hit a bridge crossing the Seine. There were a few of them so they should have got the job done easily, but they managed to miss. So as soon as we got back we were fitted with our 500lb bombs and sent back out to finish the job. But it wouldn't be the last time I would see that bridge.'

While the spring had been relentless, it was nothing compared to what he would face on 6 June, D-Day. As dawn broke, Maurice was hurtling across the English Channel, looking down on the thousands of ships heading towards the Normandy beaches. The sky was full with other Allied fighters, bombers and gliders taking the airborne troops to be dropped behind enemy lines. And as the ramps of the landing craft dropped, thousands of what looked like tiny ants poured on to the beaches and started the push into occupied Europe.

'It was quite a sight, something I will never forget. It was a very busy day indeed.'

That morning Maurice had a 500lb bomb strapped to the underside of his Spitfire, with his target one of the major rail yards. Once destroyed he returned to base for a refuel before going back out again. For the next few days Maurice and his squadron patrolled the beaches to protect the invading troops from aerial attacks, whilst also looking for targets on the ground to weaken the enemy's defences.

'It is not something I like to talk about. To think of all those people on the ground who were killed, it's not nice at all. But we got through D-Day and the days after. I remember one sortie in particular was quite something. We had to take Lancaster bombers over to target the E-Boat base at Le Havre. I hadn't done a lot of operational night flying, so that was really quite terrifying to see the flak shooting up into the sky around us. Those Bomber Command lads had that every night so I have a lot of respect for them.'

Maurice hoped that after D-Day the operations would become a little less frequent. But with the Americans and British pushing the enemy further back towards Germany, there was no chance of that. Sorties continued on a daily basis, with often two or three operations in the space of twenty-four hours. Such was the frequency that the squadron relocated to a temporary airfield in northern France where engineers laid a special track to create a makeshift runway.

A typical day would see Maurice go on a couple of sorties in the morning targeting enemy ground troops before landing at their French base for fuel and ammunition. Then in the afternoon he would go out again before flying back to RAF Lympne in the evening. The flying hours soon started to build up and, on account of his experience, he was even chosen as part of a fighter escort for the king and Prime Minister Winston Churchill, who were going over to the beaches of Normandy. But the special assignment ended up being one of his last as, on 14 August 1944, his luck finally ran out.

'I remember we had gone along to escort a group of American bombers to a target near Paris before returning to base. We went for lunch and then not long after were sent back out and told to patrol near Argentan, south of Caen.'

As soon as the squadron arrived at Argentan, there were numerous ground units for them to target and Maurice swooped down to strafe a line of tanks. But as he pulled up, there was a 'terrific bang' under his feet, which caused his knee to jolt up and hit him in the chin. Momentarily dazed, he composed himself before he felt a strange sensation in his legs. When he looked down he saw flames licking up towards his knees.

'I was doing a good 350mph so I didn't have much time to react. I didn't really feel anything, I was just thinking "I need to get the hell out of here as soon as possible".'

Despite the inferno in the cockpit, his engine was still working fine and so he pulled up to 3,000ft so his parachute would have enough time to slow him down before he hit the ground. He followed his training and reached up for the little black handle on the side of the cockpit, which when yanked released the canopy. With his legs now on fire, he pulled as hard as he could but the canopy would not budge. He tried it again but it was jammed.

By this point not only was Maurice concerned about the damage the flames were doing to his legs, he was also worried what state his parachute was in. With the flames rising and the Spitfire falling, he finally managed to rip the canopy off and release the harness holding him in. He flipped the Spitfire on its back, shifted the controls forward and dropped out of the cockpit. As he tumbled towards the earth his Mark IX exploded behind him. He pulled the ripcord, praying his parachute was still in one piece.

'I felt a huge jerk on my body and then it opened in a big white dome above me. It was the most glorious feeling. My legs were badly burnt, as was my face, my eyebrows have never fully grown back. But despite that I felt a calm, there was a great silence that was only broken by the strange sound of a skylark. I have no idea where it came from, but that was all I could hear, it was beautiful.'

Maurice floated towards the earth with no fear or pain – he was in a world of his own. That was until the morning song of the skylark was interrupted by the sound of rifle fire.

'In the field below there was a troop of German soldiers shooting at me. There was nothing I could do and the bullets were whizzing past. Thankfully they missed, but when I landed the soldiers surrounded me in seconds.'

In surviving the jump Maurice had become a member of the exclusive Caterpillar Club, so called because the early parachutes were made from silk thread. On entering the club members are given a caterpillar pin badge, which Maurice still wears proudly on the lapel of his jacket.

His trusty Spitfire, which had seen him through so many hairy situations, crashed nearby shortly before his landing. More than seventy years on archeologists are now searching for the Mark IX and had promised to take Maurice over to be reunited with it.

Maurice was now a prisoner of war, but despite having given them hell over the last few months, Maurice found his captors surprisingly pleasant. Not only that, he also found them funny.

'I remember there was lots of stomping around and clicking of heels and Heil Hitler this, Heil Hitler that. We had heard about this sort of thing, but I couldn't believe they actually did it. I couldn't help but burst out laughing.'

But the laughing soon stopped when an officer approached on a motorbike sidecar. Maurice was told to get in and he was taken to a nearby farmhouse with the officer's Luger pressed against his temple.

'I was in quite a bit of pain because I had a bit of shrapnel in my foot from the flak and also nasty burns to my legs and my face. There was no medic or anything like that and they placed me in this room with a guard who was cutting a loaf of bread. When I looked closer I could see it was covered in mould but the solider went ahead and ate it. I was looking at him in horror and he offered me a slice. I refused, having had my RAF meal shortly before, but little did I know that in a few weeks' time I would have given my right arm for a bit of that bread.'

Minutes later another soldier marched into the room. Dressed in black with a skull and crossbones badge on his uniform, Maurice quickly identified him as an SS officer. He took Maurice away and interrogated him, demanding he reveal where the rest of his crew were.

'I don't know why he was asking that, he must have known I was a Spitfire pilot, my aircraft had come down nearby. Under the rules of the Geneva Convention I only had to state my name, rank and number, but he wasn't accepting it. He was quite nasty and started waving his Luger around rather excitedly.'

Maurice had to be careful; he had heard rumours of what the SS were capable off. He was obviously concerned for his wellbeing, but at the same time he did not want to give anything away that could jeopardise the safety of his comrades. In an attempt to take the situation into his own hands, he interrupted the now furious SS officer, and asked if a doctor could take a look at his injured foot. Seemingly incensed by the question, the officer stormed out of the room and never returned.

'I had managed to get out of that tricky spot, but my foot was giving me a great deal of bother with a nasty piece of shrapnel in my instep. It didn't look like I was going to get any medical attention so I decided to do something about it. In our flying boots we had a little knife tucked into the lining. I pulled that out and then used it to cut into my foot and get the piece of shrapnel out. It hurt like anything, it was not nice at all, but I had to do it. It took a while to heal but it was much better after that.'

Maurice was not to stay at the farmhouse long and that night he was loaded into the back of a truck with a group of Canadian prisoners. Relieved to finally see some friendly faces, he was bemused that when he tried to start a conversation he was roundly ignored. He tried again, but still he got the cold shoulder. It turned out the soldiers, who had been captured at the Battle of Falaise, thought Maurice was an undercover German stooge and so were reluctant to give anything away.

The prisoners were taken across France and towards Germany, during which time Maurice won their trust. But while his relationship with the Canadians was improving, his relationship with the Germans was going the other way. Maurice and his fellow Spitfire pilots were known to the Germans as *terrorfliegers* (translated as terror fliers) due to their constant ground attacks and strafing of troops and tanks, which killed dozens each day. As such, his captors would not think twice about a rifle butt to the face or a boot in the back.

'It did get quite nasty I've got to say, but there was nothing I could really do to defend myself. I just stayed out of the way as best I could. The Canadians were very good and when we were moving as a group they would surround me for protection. It wasn't nice to be honest, I never knew what was going to happen next.'

The men continued east, before arriving in a village in Normandy where the locals had come out with food and drink. It was not a reception they had expected, but the prisoners concluded the guards must have been bribed with bottles of the local wine.

'I was standing there eating when a French man from the village came and introduced himself and handed me a bottle of Calvados. He told me that he was from the Resistance and that tonight he would get me out. I thought that was it, I thought I would be going home. But not long after an SS officer arrived in a jeep. He was furious that we had stopped and we were getting food. He pulled out his pistol and started shouting at the guards. Then he got in the jeep and ran over the food, knocking over one of the villagers in the process. We were rushed off and that's the last I saw of the village. I have been back in the years since to say thank you to the people, who could not have had much themselves. But I never managed to find it.'

Still with his bottle of Calvados, which he remembers 'went down very nicely', Maurice and the group continued into Germany on foot, travelling by night for fear of being strafed by the RAF during daylight hours. With not much food between them, the men started to tire as they reached the Seine. The Germans had taken them to what they thought was a crossing in the river and as they approached Maurice had a strange sense of déjà vu. As he got closer he was certain that he had been there before. Then as they came to the water's edge, it clicked. It was the bridge he had destroyed weeks earlier after the American bombers failed to do the job.

After a stop off in Amiens, 70 miles east of Dieppe, they moved on to Douai, just south of Lille, where Maurice was incensed at what he considered foul play by the Germans.

'It was strictly against the Geneva Convention, but they were using trucks marked with red crosses on them to transport ammunition. There was a rule that you would not attack trucks bearing a red cross and on many occasions I pulled away when I saw them on the ground. They were doing it right in front of us, it was not on.'

For the final leg into Germany, the thirty-odd men were loaded into the back of a carriage meant for just six. The cramped and uncomfortable conditions were only made worse by the two buckets in the corner – one for water and the other for everything else. After some six weeks on the road, he was separated from his Canadian Army friends, and taken to the RAF prisoner camp Stalag Luft III, which he would later discover had been the scene of the Great Escape six months earlier. But just weeks after his arrival, a dozen or so of the men, including Maurice and his good friend Peter Clarke who had also been shot down, were transferred to a nearby high-security camp. The conditions were basic to say the least and the prisoners slept in chicken sheds with no bunks or bedding. However, the main concern for the men was the lack of food. Their daily ration consisted of a loaf of bread between four. They were also given a handful of potatoes between them and a pint of soup made from turnip tops, which Maurice remembers as being 'particularly horrible'.

When they were lucky they would get soup made from dried peas, which often had a strange meaty taste owing to the presence of weevils in the broth. Then about twice a week they would get an ounce of margarine, jam made from beet-root, roasted acorn coffee and tea. It was barely enough to keep the men going and they relied on the Red Cross parcels for extra provisions. These parcels were supposed to come each week, although in reality they generally arrived about once a fortnight and would usually be shared between four.

'They really kept us going and in particular the American parcels. They would have all sorts like Spam, packets of raisins, milk powder, coffee, processed cheese and cigarettes. So short were we on food that we would have to trade – mainly cigarettes – with the guards in return for bread or whatever else they had. I remember I was so hungry one week that I swapped my watch for two loaves. I was delighted at the time but have regretted it since because I liked that watch very much.'

Officers were not required to work in the camps and so Maurice and his companions entertained themselves in whatever way they could. In particular, he took great interest in a fellow airman who had been a physiotherapist before the war. He taught Maurice the basics of the profession and gave practical lessons in the healing methods of massage. Like most things, Maurice took to it very quickly and used his new-found skill on his fellow prisoners, especially those who had suffered bad burns.

'There was a New Zealander who had been in a pretty bad state. His burns were particularly nasty and his hand was so badly burnt that it was like a claw. I managed to scrounge some oil off one of the guards and I did what I could for this chap. Remarkably, after a few goes, his hand improved and he managed to use it again.'

While to the guards it looked like Maurice and his friends were spending their hours playing bridge and giving each other massages, plans were also afoot for a breakout. Like in the Great Escape just months before, tunnellers had been working away using slats from the beds to support the passage. With Christmas approaching the tunnel was nearing completion, but the men had the problem of where they were going to dispose of all the sandy subsoil.

Given the freezing conditions the men proposed building an ice rink between two of the barracks. The commandant agreed and as the building commenced the men carefully disposed of the soil from the tunnel in and around the earth that was dug up for the rink.

All was in place for the escape, but Maurice was having reservations. He was desperate to get home and did not want to be separated from his mates. However, there was one thing stopping him: he was claustrophobic. He decided to hang on at the camp with the promise of a fresh batch of Red Cross parcels arriving for Christmas. But just days later the men were called to the parade ground where they were addressed by the commandant. With the weather outside oppressively cold, he told the men they were to head west into the snow to distance themselves from the advancing Russians. Knowing they would not last long in the conditions with little food, water or shelter, the prisoners told the commandant that they would wait and take their chances with the Red Army.

'The commandant, who was a decent man actually by comparison, gave us no choice. He stood there and got out an order that had come direct from Hitler's headquarters. It instructed him to kill all the prisoners and then return to Berlin as quickly as possible. So reluctantly we packed up what we had, put all our clothes on and prepared for this forced march which had no end destination.'

Having already endured a forced march through France, albeit in rather more favourable weather conditions, Maurice had some idea of what he would face over the coming weeks. With his good friend Peter by his side, he always tried to position himself near the front of the group. This way he would get the best chance of shelter at night and also be able to scrounge any edible plants, vegetables or anything else he might spot in the surrounding fields.

'I was something of a botanist so I knew what would be safe to eat and what wasn't. It was usually things like vegetables, some grasses, plants and things like that. It was never anything special, but because there was so little food given to us by the Germans, the stuff we foraged kept us alive.'

Maurice's knowledge of what the forest floor could offer not only prevented him from starving, it also saved his friends. But perhaps even more vital to his survival was a piece of metal he found at the start of the march. About 10in by 10in in size, the dirty piece of metal had perhaps been a lid or even a plate. But Maurice had different plans for it. With no water on the march, but with snow all around them, he decided to shape it into a pan, which he would secure above a fire made from dried grass and then melt the snow for the men to drink.

'It's funny the little things that save your life, but that really did. It was incredibly important to me and I have kept it to this day.'

They did not know it at the time but they were not alone in their journey, with more than 80,000 other prisoners from across the Third Reich heading west, away from the Russians. The winter of 1944/45 would go down as one of the coldest on record with the mercury plunging to -40°C and the winds from the north battering the already weak men. There was no ready supply of food and water and they relied on scrounging or catching whatever they could find. Rat became something of a delicacy and so hungry were the men that they even chewed on grass as they trudged along each day.

If the cold did not kill them, it was the spread of disease, with dysentery rife among the ranks. With the guards' rifles trained on the men in case any tried to escape, many prisoners would choose to soil themselves rather than stop for fear of being shot. But given how cold it was, no man could afford to discard any item of clothing – no matter how filthy.

As if that was not enough, Maurice was also repeatedly picked out by the German guards for rough treatment given his status as a *terrorflieger*. He tried to hide his uniform and his friends kept him out of view when possible, but on an almost daily basis, he would get a boot or a fist for his troubles. One day he was walking along minding his own business when a rifle butt to his head knocked him for six. He recovered his senses within seconds and carried on, but little did he know the lasting impact the strike would have. Doctors would later find an arachnoid cyst had developed, from which he suffered for the rest of his life.

It is not known how many died on The March, as it became known, but it is thought that in the region of 3,000 to 5,000 perished. Maurice had walked through blizzards, violent storms and sub-zero temperatures all on little food and water. But eventually, after several weeks, he arrived at a camp, which although basic, seemed like a hotel compared to what they had endured.

'I remember that on getting there we were given a meal of soup and rye bread which was the first proper meal we had had in a long time. It was something to savour. The camp was very basic though, there were no beds or bunks or anything like that. We all just slept on the floor and huddled together for warmth. However, this only increased the spread of disease and in particular the lice were rampant.'

Now April, the Russians were advancing at speed and the German guards were getting noticeably twitchy.

'One morning we got up and walked out of our huts, only to realise they had all gone, they had completely disappeared. It turned out the Russians had been just up the road and so, terrified by them, they went and left us.

'Finally, I thought, we were safe. With the war nearly over we would be sent back home and we would be reunited with our families. But to our shock, when the Red Army arrived a general told us to grab a weapon and go off and fight the Germans. We refused and stayed in the camp. We were in no condition to fight and the war was nearly over.'

Just days later, on 8 May, the Armistice was signed and all hostilities in Europe ended. For the first time in nearly a year, Maurice was a free man – or so he thought.

'We presumed we would be repatriated just like that, but it didn't happen. We were kept prisoner by the Russians for a good month after the war ended. It is not widely reported, but we were kept as pawns in the political game that was taking place across Europe.'

While it was not quite the same strict arrangements they'd had with the Germans, they were prevented from leaving by their so-called allies. It was the end of May when they were finally given orders to leave the camp and head north to the River Elbe where they were greeted by a welcome sight, the Americans.

'Surprisingly they handed us over without a fuss and after all that we were finally free. The Americans looked after us very well. We had hot showers for the first time in nearly a year, toilet paper and more food than we could possibly eat. Those first few hours were pure bliss.'

Maurice could have spent a few more nights with his American friends, but the following day, after his first sleep in a year with proper bedding and sheets, he was flown to Brussels.

'It was a month since the war had ended and we must have been among the last to be repatriated, but still the civilians came out and gave us a fantastic welcome, it was incredible. We were debriefed, washed down and de-loused and then given these vouchers to take to the bank.'

Unsure as to what the vouchers entitled them to, Maurice and Peter went to the counter and handed over the slips of paper. They were delighted when the cashier came back with the equivalent of £10 to spend on the town.

'We did just that and we were accosted by two beautiful English WAAFs (Women's Auxiliary Air Force) who asked if we would take them out. Of course we said yes and off we went. We drank and danced the night away; it was fantastic, especially after what we had been through the last year. I'm not sure how good my dancing was mind, as I still had my flight boots, which had been repaired by the Germans with wooden slats and nails. Anyway, after an enjoyable night, we said our goodbyes to the two WAAFs and arranged to meet with them the following day.'

The pair woke the next morning and got themselves ready to meet the girls when they received orders to make for a nearby airfield. To their disappointment they were told to board a Lancaster bomber and head home.

'I remember we landed at RAF Duxford where we were met by a squadron leader who told us, "Jolly good show chaps" and all that sort of thing. A woman from the WI then gave us a packet of Woodbines, chocolate and a shaving kit and we were given a travel card.

'I will always remember going to get the train. We must have been quite scruffy because all the civilians kept their distance. It was not like how it had been in Brussels.'

Maurice caught the train to London and then on to Eastbourne before making the final short journey to his home in the hamlet of Langley. His parents and sisters could hardly recognise him given the weight he had lost. But finally he was home and his war was over.

'It was a difficult time, but I made it through the other side. I had loved flying the Spitfire and enjoyed being part of the squadron. But I don't like to talk about it all that much now. People think of Spitfires and the pilots going along at 350mph, looping and diving. They think of it as a glamorous job, but it wasn't. You never knew if you or your mates would be coming back. It was a kill or be killed situation each and every day. There was nothing glamorous about that. It was our job.'

Three months after this interview, Maurice Macey sadly passed away at home aged 92. As friends and families gathered at Eastbourne Crematorium for his funeral on 17 September, two Spitfires emerged from the clouds and performed a flypast in close formation.

JOHN AKEHURST DFM

THE RELUCTANT HERO

L ike many of his generation, John Akehurst spoke little about his time during the war. His family had a vague idea, but the pub landlord was not one for regaling people with his stories. His son pleaded with him to write it down, but feared that the request had fallen on deaf ears. However, just days after his death in November 2014, his family found a small notepad entitled 'Last Freight Jake's War' at his home in Peacehaven. Last Freight Jake was his nickname and scribbles in his war diary told of a fearless airman who clocked up more than 750 flying hours with Bomber Command before later serving in Winston Churchill's top secret Special Operations Executive (SOE). He had flown on numerous high-profile missions until he was shot down behind enemy lines. After two weeks on the run he was captured, but tried to fight his way off a moving train before being court-martialled by Nazi High Command. His incredible story of adventure and bravery is one fit for a Hollywood film, but it was almost lost forever.

Born in 1918 in Guilford, Surrey, John's family moved to Hellingly, near Hailsham, when he was a young boy. Unlike what was to come, his childhood was unremarkable. He attended the village church where he was a choirboy and worked as a runner on the local paper. As a teenager he was a promising cyclist and broke club records as a member of the Eastbourne Rovers, and on finishing school he worked in accounts at a brewery. But with war approaching in 1938 he answered his country's call and joined the RAF at their recruitment office in Hove. He chose to try out for Bomber Command and trained as a wireless operator and air gunner and by the summer of 1940 he found himself at RAF Eastchurch on the Isle of Sheppey, Kent. It was here he got his first real taste of the war.

He recalled the moment in his diary. 'Here nearly got killed, certainly very scared. Seventy-five German bombers at 7.30 in the morning visited us and wiped out half the drome, killed forty-five. I think I was lucky under a bed in the other hall. Helped to pick up casualties on doors and took to hospital which was overwhelmed.'

Before long he had finished his training and was ready to fly operations over Europe. His first was a raid on the German-occupied port town of Dieppe on the French coast before a second, just days later to Boulogne.

Despite the terrifyingly low survival rates of members of Bomber Command, there is no hint of fear in John's diary, quite the opposite in fact, he almost appears to enjoy it. Page after page tell of daring raids on German cities, targeting key industrial and military sites. The early months of 1941 in particular appear to have been a busy time for the 23 year old, with a number of high-profile assignments, including the sinking of the great German battleship, *Bismarck*.

The pride of the Nazi fleet, at more than 790ft in length and with a crew of 2,000, the *Bismarck* had been wreaking havoc in the Atlantic. She was involved in a fierce sea battle with HMS *Hood* and HMS *Prince of Wales* on 24 May, but managed to escape towards Brest in north-west France. Bomber Command was scrambled to finish her off and, with the help of the Royal Navy, the great battleship was sunk.

Despite being only a year into his active service, John had already gained a reputation for his skill in the air and with Winston Churchill's Special Operations Executive (SOE) recruiting, he was approached in July 1941.

The SOE, set up the year before, was a secret unit operating deep behind enemy lines across occupied Europe conducting reconnaissance, espionage and sabotage. Their aim, according to Churchill, was to 'set Europe ablaze'[35]. And that is what they did, working hand in hand with the likes of the French Resistance. They were supported by a crack team from the RAF, with only the best of the best chosen for the job and assigned to 138 Squadron, which operated out of airbases at Newmarket and Stradishall in Suffolk and Tempsford in Bedfordshire.

Using modified regular bombers such as the Whitley, Lysander, Halifax and Stirling, the aircrews flew agents, explosives, radio sets and other equipment into enemy territory. The special squadron was also used to transport prominent people in top secret, including politicians and generals. Very few knew of the organisation's existence and, given the wartime leader's role in its formation, it became known as Churchill's Secret Army.

One of the missions John speaks about in his diary was among the SOE's most high profile and indeed successful of the war: the assassination of Reinhard Heydrich, one of the architects of the Holocaust. Otherwise known as the Butcher of Czechoslovakia, Heydrich was one of Hitler's right-hand men and he had personally helped organise the mass deportation and killing of millions of Jews from German-occupied territory. He was later appointed the acting Reich Protector of what is now the Czech Republic.

Described by the Führer as the 'man with the iron heart', he was ruthless and brutal in his methods. He sought to eliminate opposition to the Nazi occupation by suppressing Czech culture and deporting and executing anyone who resisted. He was also responsible for the Einsatzgruppen, a special task force that followed in the wake of the German Army and killed more than 1 million people, including countless Jews.

He was a key target for the Allies, but given his seniority he was heavily protected and well out of reach of any army. It was decided that this was a job for the SOE. Back in London a plan was drawn up to fly two specially trained agents, Jozef Gabčík and Jan Kubiš, into Prague to carry out the attack. John and his crew were to transport the Czech Assassins, as they were to be known.

After months of preparation the order was given on the evening of 21 December 1941, and the two operatives scrambled aboard John's Halifax bomber at Tangmere Airport, near Chichester. Shortly before 10 p.m. they took off, travelling without an escort in the hope they would not be spotted by anti-aircraft gun crews or German night fighters. The journey started smoothly and they flew over the French coast at Le Crotoy before heading towards Germany. But just after 12.30 a.m. Luftwaffe fighters intercepted them over Darmstadt. The Halifax's pilot ducked and weaved, returned fire and thankfully saw them off.

They continued on towards Prague and as they flew over what they believed to be the drop zone, the two assassins parachuted in. But the heavy snow saw them miss their intended target with the men instead landing near a village called Nehvizdy near Čelákovice, east of the capital.

While Gabčík and Kubiš gathered up their chutes and made for cover, John and the crew turned for home, only to come under fire again as they flew back over Darmstadt, this time from anti-aircraft guns. They rode their luck through the flak and landed back at Tangmere at just past 8 a.m. the following morning.

Meanwhile Gabčík and Kubiš were meeting up with contacts in their homeland and planning their attack. They had received specialist training from both the Scots Guards and explosives experts at the SOE and were equipped with a deadly arsenal of weapons. But the pair were not going to be rushed and it was five months before they picked their moment. They were to ambush the high-ranking Nazi as he made his daily commute through the capital. They picked a tight corner in the road where his driver would have to slow down and they would be waiting at a nearby tram stop – armed to the teeth.

On the morning of 27 May 1942, Heydrich's convertible Mercedes 320 slowed for the corner as expected and Gabčík stepped in front of the vehicle and pulled out his Sten machine gun. Pointing it straight at Heydrich, he squeezed the trigger, only for it to jam. Heydrich pulled out his pistol and started shooting at Gabčík. Realising his friend was in trouble, Kubiš threw one of his specially modified sensitive impact fuse grenades towards the car, sending shrapnel flying through the air. The explosion injured both Kubiš and crucially Heydrich.

The assassins made their getaway and with the car out of action, Heydrich and his driver pursued them on foot. But the injured Heydrich soon collapsed. He was taken to a nearby hospital and operated. He looked to be recovering when, on 3 June, while sitting in bed eating breakfast, he slipped into a coma and died the following day. The mission had been a success, but Hitler was furious and ploughed copious resources into finding and killing the two assassins.

The SS tracked down those who had assisted them and they were tortured and killed. Gabčík and Kubiš, meanwhile, were traced to a church in Prague where they had been hiding with other members of the Resistance movement. For fourteen hours they held out in a bloody battle, killing fourteen German soldiers. But the church was eventually overrun, and Kubiš and Gabčík were pushed back into the crypt where they staged their last stand. Kubiš was hit and died of blood loss while Gabčík, who was running out of ammunition, chose suicide over being captured and shot himself. [36]

The assassination was one of many SOE operations in which John played a crucial part. While they did not involve taking huge swathes of land or defeating great armies, they helped turn the tide of the war.

His flying hours soon started to rack up and, given the grim prognosis for Bomber Command members, recruits were told that after a certain number of sorties they would be reassigned to a less dangerous role. John was approaching his limit in late 1941 and so proposed to his sweetheart, Joyce. They married in September, but the head of Bomber Command, Arthur Harris, could not let one of his best men go and so called him back up. Not long after he was awarded the Distinguished Flying Medal for his bravery and courage.

While continuing with his SOE duties, John flew numerous Bomber Command operations up to mid-1942 and helped spearhead some of the first major bombing raids on German cities, including Cologne and Essen. His skills were so in demand, that with the war less than three years in, he had already clocked more time in the skies than most, with his logbook showing in excess of 750 hours.

However, unbeknown to him at the time, his final operation was to be on the evening of 13 September 1942. John and his crew set off in their Wellington from RAF Steeple Morden, in Cambridgeshire, bound for Bremen in the north-west of Germany. They were not alone and were joined by 446 other aircraft in a huge raid on the industrial heart of the city, with a particular focus on the Focke-Wulf fighter plane factory.

The raid was a success, putting the factory out of action and leaving other industry significantly damaged. More than seventy on the ground were killed and nearly 400 injured, while close to 850 houses were destroyed.[37]

With their bombs dropped, John's Wellington, piloted by his friend, Flying Officer Michael Dickenson, turned for home. But over the town of Lingen, close to the border of Holland, they were intercepted by German night fighters. They took a direct hit and one of the engines caught fire. The crew tried desperately to keep the bomber in the air to make it over the English Channel. John recalled the moment in his diary. 'We would have one engine if we could put out the fire … but I think it was a bit optimistic. This proved right. I went back and started throwing out anything that could be jettisoned.'

But it was no use, the bomber was going down and the pilot radioed his crew to tell them to bail out. When there was no response he realised that the intercom had been destroyed by the flak and so, unwilling to abandon his crew, he prepared to crash-land the stricken Wellington in a swamp.

'The next thing I remember was an almighty bang,' John wrote, 'and where I was standing seemed to explode. I went head over heels in the aircraft. The fire in the engine and the wing then burst out more fiercely. I was trapped in the fuselage; there was a fire in the front and no way out of the back. I knew that there was a small escape hatch on the side of the aircraft but it was buried in earth. Sticking my hand into the earth I could feel cool air. The next thing I remember I was standing at the side of the burning aircraft which by now was so intense.'

John, who must have been hauled from the burning wreckage by one of his fellow crewmembers, was shaken but uninjured. Miraculously all five survived the crash-landing and the men dusted themselves down and prepared to set off on foot.

After the war had ended John discovered the poignant entry in his flight log, recording this final mission: 'Opperations Bremen [sic], failed to return' it read.

'It was the end of my flying career in the RAF,' he reflected in his diary, 'and a new chapter to start.'

With German aircraft circling overhead looking for survivors, the five decided to split up and attempt to make their way back to England. John and the pilot, Flying Officer Dickenson, shook hands with the other three and wished them luck before heading off west by the stars. They walked in silence, knowing that German soldiers would have been sent out to round up any survivors. After no more than thirty minutes they heard shouting and ran for cover, fearing the worst. The other three had managed to walk across a German anti-aircraft gun crew and were captured.

The pair had just one escape kit between them, which contained four squares of chocolate, water-cleaning tablets and a basic map. By day they hid in woodland areas and then walked by night. Yet this was slow and agonising progress, as John recalled in his diary. 'Have you ever tried to walk across country in the dark in a straight line? Well I can assure you it consists of walking a few hundred yards and then coming across a hedge or barbed wire, water or trees. This we did for two nights, but now the weather took a turn and decided to make things not so pleasant. The second night we hid to sleep but a storm came over suddenly and this caused some of the village children to dash for shelter right on top of us. They gave a yell and ran off.'

Within minutes they could hear the sound of the German equivalent of the local Home Guard and their dogs bearing down on them. They had to move quickly, and decided to try hiding in a ditch by the side of the road. One of the dogs ran ahead and found them, but the owner did not notice until it was too late and the pair managed to escape.

They continued to rest in the day and move by night for much of the next week, still having not eaten since they left England. One evening they came across a railway and followed it until they heard a train pulling into a nearby station. They decided to try and hitch a lift, but as they approached the carriages, the train pulled out. The pair crawled across the platform and waited in the shadows for another train, but with no sign of any activity, they decided to cut their losses and made for a copse of trees where they spent the rest of the night.

Becoming increasingly weak from lack of food, they took the risk of walking nearer to the main roads to take advantage of the signs, which had been left in place – unlike those back in England. They soon found themselves near the town of Papenburg, just 15 miles from the Dutch border and that night decided they would make a dash for it.

'Setting off we soon came to a row of cottages near a power station and after doing a reconnaissance, decided to press on through towards the small town of Papenburg. As we continued through, a person came out of a gate in front of a home, we could not do anything but walk on. Mike called out *"Guten nacht"* (good night in German) and got some reply. This meant we now were vulnerable and had to dive into a garden for half an hour. On proceeding after this time we suddenly realised we were being followed so carried on walking. What we did not realise was that waiting for us a little further on was a police car. We were caught between the two groups.'

After ten days on the run together with no food and little water, the pair had come agonisingly close to making it over the border, where the Dutch Resistance would have aided their journey home. But just miles short they had been caught by the German civil police force. Unarmed, there was no question of trying to fight their way out of the situation and so they went quietly – at least for the time being.

In his diary, John recalled the moment the game was up. 'Much shouting of "hands hock" and other words. We were placed in a VW Beetle and on the way to the jail in Papenburg. Mike and I had our pockets emptied and our boots and belts taken and put in a cell. Halfway through the night the policeman came into the cell and took me out. I wondered why, but it was because Mike was an officer and I was an NCO. In the German Army this is very rigid, they enforce this very much.'

Expecting the worst, the pair awoke the following morning unsure of what treatment to expect. But they could hardly believe their eyes when the policeman came to unlock their cells carrying their first meal in ten days. The officer, it turned out, had a son in the Luftwaffe, and given the mutual respect between the two flying forces, he was only too happy to help the downed airmen. Later the same day, allegiances were well and truly thrown out the window when, on learning it was Flying Officer Dickenson's twenty-first birthday, one of the police officer's wives baked him a cake.

But the pleasantries would soon come to an end when two soldiers turned up to transport them to a prisoner-of-war camp. However, John and Mike had different ideas and they hatched a plan to jump their guards on the train and escape. As the service approached the city of Aachen, near the border with Belgium, Mike leapt to his feet and took on one of the guards. John is said to have taken a flying kick at the other before the pair made for the door of the moving train. But with Mike still brawling with his guard, they were soon wrestled back into their seats.

Recalling the incident in his diary, John wrote: 'He whispered to me "When I stand up make for the door of the train and jump out". Easier said than done.

Mike got engaged with his guard and I could not jump without Mike. From now on we spent all the time with our hands on our heads and at the next station more guards came into the carriage.' The situation, John coolly put it, 'became tense'.

Their insubordinate attempt to escape would not be forgotten by their captors. That night the pair were locked up at a Luftwaffe aerodrome. The following morning they continued on their journey by train to Dulag Luft, a transit prisoner-of-war camp near the town of Oberursel close to Frankfurt.

It was officially just a processing camp but allegations of torture during interrogation were made by prisoners there.[38] In his diary John makes mention of 'days of questioning' and 'lots of shouting' with 'very little food to bring you to heel'. After trying to get him to fill out one of the counterfeit Red Cross forms drawn up by the German Intelligence, they wanted a full and detailed explanation of the train incident. They were then transported, this time with more guards, to Stalag VIIIB near Łambinowice in the south-west of what is now Poland.

On arriving at the camp, they were tied up by their hands and left all day. John later discovered this punishment was in retaliation for what Canadian troops did to German prisoners following the failed Dieppe raid in August 1942. The conditions in the camp were poor and with the men stripped of their warm flying boots and jackets, replaced only with wooden clogs and blankets, the Eastern European winds chilled them to the bone.

But John was not to be there long. The Nazis were looking to make an example of him for the escape attempt and he was transferred to Stalag Luft III – the scene of the Great Escape – pending a court martial. Despite its reputation, John found the camp more than agreeable.

'Here the treatment was like a three-star hotel compared with 8B. I was given clothing, boots, washing and shaving cream, knife, fork and spoon. None of this was available at 8B. All I had when I was there was a tin can to drink out of and eat off when flattened.'

But the welcome he received from his fellow prisoners was not as pleasant. With plans for escape well underway, the men were acutely paranoid about German spies infiltrating their ranks.

John talks of being met by elected camp leader RAF Sergeant James Dixie Deans before being interrogated. It was only when he came across one of his friends in the camp, who vouched for him, the suspicion was dropped.

He settled into camp life, sharing stories with his fellow airmen until, on 7 December 1942, when guards pulled him to one side and marched him off at gunpoint to the 'Cooler'. He was to be held in the camp's solitary confinement for his actions on the train, prior to his court martial. Unlike the 1963 movie though, there was no baseball and glove, instead it was cards, crayons and an improvised game of battleships.

'Although it was solitary confinement, after some time I was able to come out of the cell in the evenings when the senior NCO was not there enjoying a coffee and a chat with the guards. One evening I was in an adjoining cell playing cards with another POW when the Sergeant came back.

'I remember playing battleships, the game when you have a number of squares on a piece of paper … this was done via a hole in the water piping with the cell next door. I also spent my time with crosswords from the camp and drawing on the wall of my cell with crayons. We were sent these to draw on paper but I decorated my cell with big drawings. Then one day I was visited by the Swiss Red Cross.'

The Germans had wanted to make an example of John for his escape attempt in an effort to prevent others from following his lead. He was to be court-martialled by the Nazi High Command, one of the first Allied prisoners to receive such treatment.

He was transported under armed guard to Dresden where the regional head-quarters of the Luftwaffe was. After being held in an underground dungeon, as John remembered it in his diary, which he simply described as a 'really terrible place', he was hauled before the military court.

'I have never seen so many high-ranking officers and Swastikas – quite impressive,' he remarked.

The process was all by the book, or at least it gave this impression, and John and Mike, his co-accused, were given a Swiss Red Cross lawyer to represent them while a German lawyer would present the case against. They were also introduced to a smartly turned out South African man, who they were told would also act as a legal representative for them.

John went to shake hands and Mike introduced the man as Squadron Leader Roger Bushell. The name meant nothing to him at the time, but Bushell, he would later discover, was the Big X at Stalag Luft III and the mastermind of the Great Escape.

The Spitfire pilot had studied law at Pembroke College, Cambridge, and so was hauled from the camp to represent the pair. Bushell, who at the time of the proceedings would have been planning the Great Escape, was one of fifty executed by the Gestapo following the breakout in the spring of 1944.

But even with Bushell's help, the pair were shown no leniency and were given a nine-month prison sentence. Given their current prisoner status, the punishment may not have appeared too arduous. But where they were to be sent was far worse than any prisoner-of-war camp they had experienced before. Their destination was Grudziądz in the north of Poland, about 60 miles to the south of the port city of Danzig, now Gdańsk, in Poland.

Grudziądz was home to a military prison, primarily holding Polish activists, but also used to house troublemaking British prisoners of war. The guards at the prison had a reputation for mistreatment and there were rumours that inmates were not making it to the end of their sentences. For John, it was where he spent some of the darkest days of the war.

'I now know what prison conditions are like,' he recalled, 'back to clogs and in a solitary cell twenty-three hours a day. No looking out the barred window, no laying on the mattress, which I found had bed bugs, and prison rations of one litre of soup a day consisting of pea pods, potato peelings and hot water plus one large slice of bread.'

The conditions were brutal and, with no toilets in their cells, they had to ask the guards to be taken out if they needed to answer the call of nature. Most of the other Allied prisoners were army personnel who had been caught with women while out of their camps and supposed to be working. At the regular prisoner-of-war camps, army and RAF personnel were housed separately, with the Luft camps run by the Luftwaffe for the airmen and the army camps run by their corresponding service. In many of the army camps, there was the option to head out of the main compound, under guard, and work in the nearby towns and factories.

John, who always had plans for escape in mind, expressed his disbelief at the lack of imagination and desire, as he put it, of his armed forces comrades.

'I can never understand how the thousands of army POWs who had to go out to work did not take the chances of escape. In the Luft POW camps the hardest job was to get out: the barbed wire guarded with machine guns, searchlights, dogs day and night. The army had it on a plate.'

At Grudziądz, John had few comforts and each day was something of an ordeal. The one ray of light for most men was a smoking parade when they were given two cigarettes to enjoy. They were strictly forbidden from taking them back to their cells and were strip searched to prevent them from doing so. However, ever resourceful, John hatched an ingenious plan to ensure that he could enjoy a smoke in his own time. He first took apart the cigarette and smuggled it back past the guards on his person. He then managed to get some flint from one of the Polish prisoners and snapped off a piece of razor blade, which they were issued with twice a week for shaving. After taking apart his toothbrush, which in those days were flammable, he struck the blade against the flint and lit part of his brush. The tobacco, which he had smuggled in, was rolled up in a piece of paper and he had himself a lit cigarette.

Little victories like this kept his sprits up and after nine months of near-constant solitary confinement he was released and transported 40 miles south to his fifth prisoner-of-war camp, Stalag XX-A in Toruń, also in Poland.

Such was his relief that he described the day of his release – 7 December 1943 – in his diary as 'freedom day'. Stalag XX-A was a huge camp which at its peak held as many as 20,000 men, mostly army personnel, some of whom had been there since their capture at Dunkirk. Although basic, it was like a hotel compared to what John had endured for the past nine months.

Unlike John's previous camps, prisoners were allowed to go out and work in the nearby farms and towns, in return for extra food and privileges. However, to his disappointment, the commandant would only let the army prisoners out while John and one other airman were forced to stay behind. Each day he would see the prisoners come back with eggs, soap, bread and even vodka hidden down their trousers. He decided that he wanted some of the action, so one day he swapped uniforms with a soldier.

'I went out with a digging party, the guard knew I was not supposed to be there but was not concerned. We marched out of camp with spades, forks and pick axes into town. When we got to the tunnel they were digging they threw their tools in the trench and just went shopping. This was done all the time. The poor old airmen in the Luft camps never saw an egg, booze or fruit at any time.'

But there was more to life in Stalag XX-A than first met the eye, as while the Germans tried to control the men's trade of food and alcohol, an escape plan was being hatched. John was approached and asked if he wanted to be part of it, which, of course, he did. They were to set off before Christmas, following an escape route which would take them through to Sweden.

'I was fixed up with a passport and papers to travel, all forged with all the stamps just like real ones. An amount of genuine money was sewn into my jacket and a fellow … and I got together to be ready to leave at a minute's notice.'

All was in place with John confident of making it home. But at the eleventh hour the would-be escapees in front of him in the line were caught and he was told to hold back and wait for another opportunity. That opportunity never came, as on Christmas Eve he was called out in parade once more and told he was to be transported to another camp, this time to the northern-most part of Nazi-occupied Europe, to Heydekrug or Stalag Luft VI, in what is now Šilutė in Lithuania.

It was here he met and grew close to an American who was flying with the RAF, Flight Sergeant Luke Davidson. He, like John, was not content to sit out the war as a prisoner and so tried it on with the Germans. His plan was to convince the camp doctor he had gone deaf. It worked, and he was sent to Sweden to be repatriated.

To pass the hours at Heydekrug, John took to his scrapbook, drawing cartoons, camp scenes and aircraft. One such drawing shows the camp's theatre, which the prisoners helped build and was used to stage plays. Other sketches show the guard towers and his hut, complete with wood panelling, stove, lockers and bunk beds. He also collected names and addresses of those he met during his time as a prisoner, presumably with the intention of keeping in touch when the war ended. Clearly popular, the addresses range from South Australia to Los Angeles and Canada. He kept his scrapbook hidden up his jumper throughout his time as a prisoner and it remains in good condition to this day.

John was at Heydekrug until January 1944, when the western advance of the Russians forced the guards to move the prisoners once again. More than 2,000 men were transported to Memel, Lithuania, and crammed in the hold of a coal barge called the *Insterburg*. So small was the space, there was no room for the men to lie down and they remained there for three days and nights. Eventually they reached the Nazi-occupied port of Peenemünde on the Baltic Sea, close to a V2 rocket research centre and so frequently a target for Allied aircraft.

When John and the rest of the men arrived, the Americans were bombing the port. With nowhere to take cover, they were tied up by the guards, handcuffed in two railway carriages and left to hope for the best. Bombs fell all around but thankfully none hit and, when the raid was over, they set off on the final leg of their journey to Stalag Luft IV, near the town of Tychowo in north-west Poland. With the camp in sight, the guards who had accompanied them from Lithuania suddenly disappeared and in their place came a group of younger-looking replacements. As they walked towards the men, John could tell by their uniform that they were members of the Hitler Youth.

The group, which dated back to the mid-1920s, was created to ensure the future of Hitler's Third Reich and the Aryan race. They were indoctrinated in the Nazi Party's ideas and beliefs from a young age and trained up to be the soldiers of the future. Despite most being under 18 years of age, their treatment of prisoners was brutal, as John was about to find out.

'We were told to march, which means run. With bayonets and dogs they chased us up the road, cutting the kit we were carrying with the bayonets and using them on the POWs. Also dogs were used. When we arrived at Luft IV it was apparent people had been stabbed and bitten by dogs and nearly all their kit removed. This we later were told was reprisals for the attempt on Hitler's life.'

The camp itself, John recalled, was not quite ready, with the toilets yet to be installed. Instead they were forced to use a long trench with poles suspended above for the men to sit on. 'Not much privacy in the open air,' he remarked.

Slowly the conditions and facilities improved and given that it was a Luft camp, it was not long before it felt like home for John. He added: 'The days went by and we noticed that the Russians had overrun an old camp and were now well on their way towards us again. Finally, in January 1944, we were told we were to be moved again, this time by boat. So we had to collect what possessions we had and be ready to walk westward at about 15 miles each day. It was snowing and very cold and some of the POWs were soon in trouble. Little did they know that this was to go on for three months up to the end of the war.'

With the Russians getting closer throughout the winter of 1944/45, Hitler ordered more than 80,000 Allied prisoners to be taken west to prevent them from being liberated. The winter turned out to be the coldest of the twentieth century, with deadly snowstorms, blizzards and temperatures plummeting to -13°F (-25°C).

There was little food and the men, already wasting away on prisoner rations, were forced to scavenge whatever they could find. Some were said to have resorted to eating cats, dogs and even rats.

Trench foot, dysentery and gangrene were widespread, and such was the lack of shelter and warm clothing that some men froze to death in their sleep. Around 3,500 died as a result of the conditions, with some estimates as high as 8,000. It came to be known as The Long March or simply The March.

'With nowhere to sleep we were lucky to get a piece of bread and some soup now and again. We slept where we could, they tried to find farm sheds. How long this lasted I cannot remember but I soon got fed up.'

John hatched a plan for escape with two of his friends from the camp: Leslie Mitchell and Tony Johnson. They waited until the guards were not looking before making a break for it.

'As we approached a forest still in thick snow, the armed guards and dogs had to close up to get through. This was our chance … we made a dash into the woods;

we expected to be fired on or the dogs to be set on us but, with our hearts beating fast, we dived into a snowdrift and waited. No response, we were free.'

That night, with snow falling heavily, they decided to stay in the trees for shelter. They could hear the shouts of the German guards nearby and so they knew they had to move soon.

As John remarks in his diary, he was resigned to the fact that their chances of survival were slim. The temperatures were sub-zero, they had no food or water and the area was crawling with soldiers. They waited as long as they could for the conditions to clear and then headed east in the hope they would find the advancing Russian Army. Day after day they trudged through the unforgiving conditions, sleeping in the snow and eating it for a source of fluids. Two weeks passed but there was still no sign of the Red Army and with his companion, Leslie Mitchell, starting to get sick, they decided to make for an aerodrome after seeing planes circling overhead.

'That night we were in a small forest of fir trees almost 10ft to 12ft high. As we lay on the freezing ground we could hear grunts and squeals as a herd of wild boar was in the same bit of wood as we were. The trees were not tall enough to climb so we had to spend all night with the wild pigs all around us. Towards the aerodrome … we passed a cottage with an old woman outside. In my best German, which was enough to get me by, I asked the way to the Luft Platz (aerodrome). She said go on to the bridge, turn right and there you are. She was right, it led us straight to the aerodrome and we entered a hangar full of FW 190 fighter planes.'

They sat and watched, pondering their next move. If they played their cards right, then this could be their way out. But they had been spotted.

'All hell let loose, shouting, everybody running, the Germans realised we were there and they did not like it. We were hauled before the German commander and questioned. I explained that we were POWs who through no fault of their own had lost their comrades and that my friend was ill. I heard the commander say "He speak a good German". Anyway it worked, we were given a nice warm cell and food.'

After about ten days they were on the move again, this time heading west to Stettin, now Szczecin in Poland, where they were thrown in a cell with two captured Russian airmen. John tried his best to communicate with the pair by 'adding ski to every word' with remarkable success. As a gesture of friendship he tore a button off his RAF-issue tunic and swapped it with his counterpart, saving this keepsake until the day he died. But they were not to be in Stettin long and were ushered out into the cold on foot again, heading north to Barth on the Baltic coast. They were being taken to yet another prisoner-of-war camp, Stalag Luft I, which was made up largely of American airmen. While many prisoners preferred to be with their fellow countrymen, John did not mind being thrown in with their friends from across the Atlantic.

'The one advantage of being with Americans was they were being highly supplied with goodies, unlike the RAF. When an airman of the USA left a Dulag interrogation centre they came away with a large suitcase of gear and plenty of clothing. When I left Dulag, I had a nice pair of size twelve clogs and not much else.'

Having been a resident at numerous camps and prisons during the war, John was always pleased to be thrown in a Luft. 'The Luftwaffe camps were the ones to look after us (thank them). Life in the camp there was good; they had stocks of Red Cross parcels and seemed to be very comfortable in every way. Thank goodness I ended up there and not with the Death March of my fellow comrades, who spent three months on the road before being shot at by friendly fighters.'

As the spring sunshine started to melt away the snow, John settled into life at Stalag Luft I. What little information they got into the camp suggested the war was coming to an end, with the Russians advancing on Berlin from the east and the Americans and British from the west.

Confirmation of what they had been hoping for came at the start of May 1945, when the guards abandoned their positions, leaving them in no-man's-land between the remaining German Army and the oncoming Red Army.

Although not yet safe, the novelty of this new-found freedom was not lost on John and, with no guards at the gates, he decided to go for a look around. Ever the adventurer, he found a yacht and decided to take some of the men out on the Baltic Sea – which was still perilously cold even in May. But with the yacht full the vessel started to list before capsizing, leaving the men treading water miles from the shoreline. Thankfully they found some logs and made a makeshift raft and paddled back to dry land.

After this mishap, John decided to wait it out until the Russians arrived and, sure enough, a few days later they heard the sound of gunfire in the distance. The locals hung white flags from their windows and, with the German guards long gone, a Russian general came galloping into town on a huge horse like a Napoleonic hero.

He gave the newly released prisoners food and horses of their own, and so John and his friends went about exploring the area, looking for souvenirs. They had no idea how long they would have to wait to be taken home, but on 5 May, with the sound of aircraft overhead, they looked to the skies hoping to see their RAF colleagues. At first the sight of the American Air Force B17 Flying Fortress left them disappointed, but on landing, the pilot told them he was there to take them home.

They piled into the back of the American four-engine bomber and flew over a devastated Western Europe towards England. John noted in his diary that, when flying above Hamburg, 'not a building was standing'. The same was true for many of Germany's major cities, given the aerial bombing of the British and Americans in the latter stages of the war.

Finally, two years and 264 days after leaving RAF Steeple Morden for their failed raid on Bremen, John set foot on home soil at Ford Aerodrome in Sussex. 'A quick shower, food and new uniforms and we were packed off home. I had not seen my wife Joyce for two years, eight months. I was then sent on indefinite leave with the promise that we could be returned to join in the Japan War, which was still going on. This never happened so I stayed home in Eastbourne until I was demobbed a year later.'

Reflecting on his remarkable war, John wrote in his diary, 'I went from junior clerk 1939 to Bomber Command … back again in 1945 to the same office in Terminus Road, Eastbourne. Had I been dreaming it all?'

John returned to his pre-war life as if the last six years had not happened. He raised a family and was later a popular pub landlord. He ran a number of hostelries, including the Hampton in Upper North Street, Brighton, in the mid-1950s, and Ye Olde Smugglers Inne in Alfriston a decade later. He had experienced more in those six years than most would in a dozen lifetimes. But the modest family man did not dine out or show off about his tales of adventure, bravery and daring. Quite the opposite – he took many of them to his grave, aged 96, in November 2014. John's is a story worthy of a feature film, and his courage and perilous love of mischief are both admirable and shocking in equal measures. With many of our remaining veterans now nearing the end of their lives, the great fear is that stories like John's will be lost forever. We cannot let this happen; their brave sacrifice should never be forgotten.

SOURCES

1. Renouf, T., *Black Watch, Liberating Europe and Catching Himmler* (Digital: London, 2011)
2. Churchill, W., *The Second Word War, Volume IV, The Hinge of Fate* (Cassell: London, 1951)
3. Middlebrook, M., *Arnhem 1944: The Airborne Battle* (Pen & Sword: Barnsley, 2009)
4. Roberts, A., *High Courage on the Axe-Edge of War. The Times*, 31 March 2007. Available from www.thetimes.co.uk. [Accessed 1 May 2015]
5. Royal Air Force, *The Thousand Bomber Raids, 30/31 May (Cologne) to 17 August 1942*. Available from www.raf.mod.uk. [Accessed 1 May 2015]
6. *Ibid.*
7. *Ibid.*
8. Klein, A., *Beyond The Battle: Fascinating Facts. The Times*, 9 July 2010. Available from www.thetimes.co.uk. [Accessed 1 May 2015]
9. Thompson, P., *The Battle for Singapore: The True Story of the Greatest Catastrophe of World War 2* (Piatkus: London, 2006)
10. Johnston, A., *Death in the Spice Islands*. Available from www.britain-at-war.org.uk/WW2/Haruku. [Accessed 22 February 2015]
11. *Ibid.*
12. Brown-Raymond, L., *Ships from Hell, Japanese War Crimes on the High Seas* (The History Press: Stroud, 2002)
13. *Ibid.*
14. *Ibid.*
15. Knappmann, E.W., *The Adolf Eichmann Trial, 1962, Great World Trials* (Gale Research: Detroit, 1997)
16. Wearth, A., *Russia at War 1941–1945* (Basic Books: New York, 1999)
17. Caddick-Adams, P., *Monte Cassino: Ten Armies in Hell* (Oxford University Press: Oxford, 2013)
18. Hapgood, D., *Monte Cassino: The Story of the Most Controversial Battle of World War II* (Da Capo Press: Boston, 2002)
19. Ellis, J., *Blackpool at War: A History of the Fylde Coast during the Second World War* (The History Press: Stroud, 2013)
20. Meserole, M., *The Great Escape: Tunnel to Freedom* (Sterling Point Books: New York, 2008)
21. Read, S., *Human Game: Hunting the Great Escape Murderers* (Constable and Robinson: London, 2013)
22. Carroll, T., *The Great Escape from Stalag Luft III* (Pocket Books: New York, 2004)
23. *Ibid.*
24. Holocaust Education and Archive Research Team, *The Breendonk Internment Camp in Belgium*. Available from www.holocaustresearchproject.org. [Accessed 4 March 2015]
25. *Ibid.*

26. Delaforce, P., *The Black Bull: From Normandy to the Baltic with the 11th Armoured Division*
    (Pen & Sword: Barnsley, 2010)
27. Dimbleby, R. *Liberation of Belsen*, BBC, 13 May 1945.
    Available from news.bbc.co.uk/1/hi/in_depth/4445811.stm. [Accessed 1 May 2015]
28. De Segundo, W., *Obituary Brigadier Robert Daniell. The Independent*, 19 December 1996.
    Available from www. independent.co.uk. [Accessed 12 May 2015]
29. Lengyel, O., *Five Chimneys: A Women Survivor's True Story of Auschwitz*
    (Academy Chicago Publishers: Chicago, 1995)
30. Bergen-Belsen, *The Trial (Defence – Evidence for the Defendant Irma Grese)*.
    Available from www.bergenbelsen.co.uk. [Accessed 25 April 2015]
31. Hedgepeth, S.M. and Saidel, R.G., *Sexual Violence against Jewish Women during the
    Holocaust* (University Press of New England: Lebanon, US, 2010)
32. Jones, P., *Quickly To Her Fate* (P.J. Publishing: Chester, 2010)
33. Lifton, R.J., *The Nazi Doctors, Medical Killing and the Psychology of Genocide*
    (Basic Books: New York, 1986)
34. Shapiro, S., *Truth Prevails: Demolishing Holocaust Denial: The End of the Leuchter Report.*
    (The Beate Klarsfeld Foundation: New York, 1990)
35. Morris, N., *The Special Operations Executive 1940–1946.* BBC.
    Available from www.bbc.co.uk/worldwars. [Accessed 20 April 2015]
36. Burian, M., Knížek, A. and Stehlík, E., *Assassination, Operation Anthropoid 1941–1942*
    (Avis: Prague, 2002)
37. *Mission Bremen*. Available from www.aircrewremembrancesociety.co.uk.
    [Accessed 25 January 2015]
38. Simmons, K., *Kriegie* (Thomas Nelson & Sons: New York, 1960)

BACKGROUND READING

Amery, J., *At the Mind's Limit: Contemplations by a Survivor on Auschwitz and its Realities*
    (Indiana University Press: Indiana, 1998)
Bennett, D., *A Magnificent Disaster: The Failure of Market Garden, The Arnhem Operation:
    September 1944* (Casemate: Drexel Hill, 2008)
Hastings, M., *Bomber Command* (Pan Macmillan: London, 1999)
Macdonald, C., *The Killing of Reinhard Heydrich* (Da Capo Press: Boston, 1998)
Nichol, J. and Rennell, T., *The Last Escape: The Untold Story of Allied Prisoners of War in Germany
    1944–1945* (Penguin: London, 2003)
Parker, M., *Monte Cassino: The Story of the Hardest-fought Battle of World War Two*
    (Headline: London, 2003)
Perl, G., *I Was A Doctor in Auschwitz* (Arno Press: New York, 1984)
Rempel, G., *Hitler's Children: The Hitler Youth and the SS* (University of North Carolina Press:
    North Carolina, 1989)
Sebag-Montefiore, H., *Dunkirk, Fight to the Last Man* (Penguin: London, 2007)

Also from The History Press

WAR IN
THE SKIES